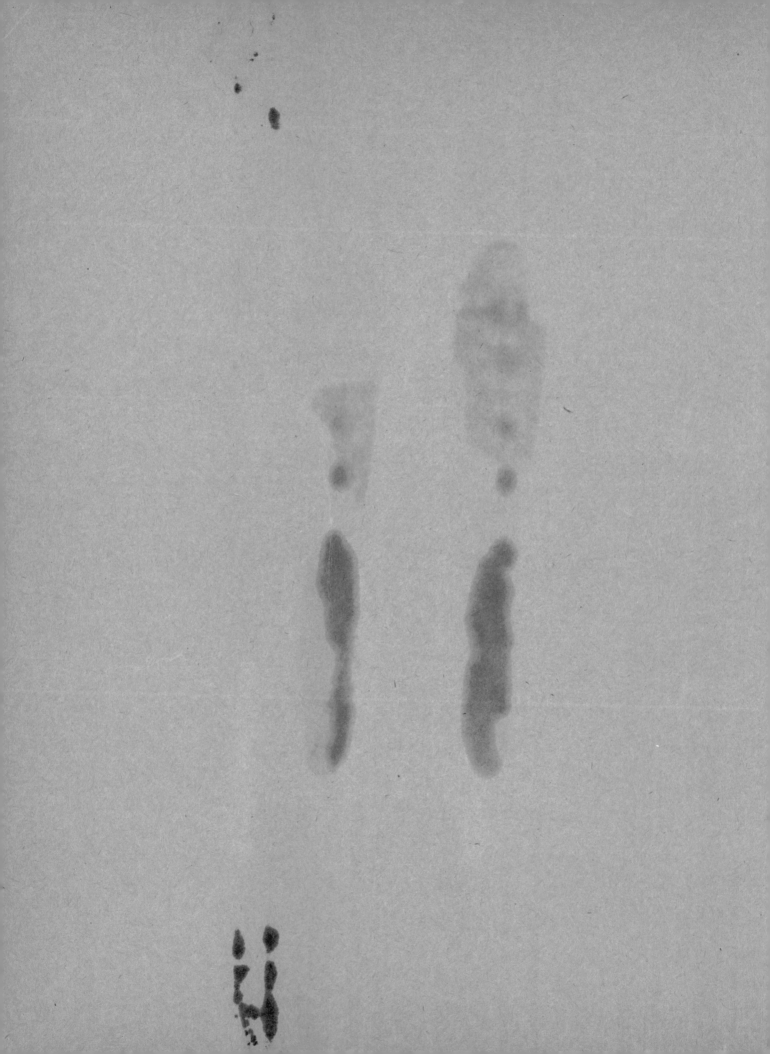

FREDERIC REMINGTON *and*
the Spanish-American War

Charge of the Rough Riders at San Juan Hill.
(Courtesy of the Remington Art Museum, Ogdensburg, New York)

FREDERIC REMINGTON and the Spanish-American War

by
Douglas Allen

CROWN PUBLISHERS, INC.   NEW YORK

Inquiries should be addressed to Crown Publishers, Inc., 419 Park Avenue South, New York, N.Y. 10016.

Library of Congress Catalog Card Number: 76-127514

Printed in the United States of America

Published simultaneously in Canada by General Publishing Company Limited

Design by Iris Kleinman

Acknowledgments

I wish to express my gratitude to those who assisted me in my effort to make this book as complete as possible: Atwood Manley of Canton, N.Y.; Dr. Foster Brown, President Emeritus, St. Lawrence University, Canton, N.Y.; Dr. Andrew K. Peters, Chief Librarian, Owen D. Young Library, St. Lawrence University; Mrs. Belnap and Mrs. Ernest J. Duval, Gouverneur, N.Y.; J. N. Bartfield, J. N. Bartfield Art Galleries, Inc., N.Y.; Rudolf Wunderlich and Eugene J. Coulon, Kennedy Galleries, Inc., N.Y.; The Metropolitan Museum of Art.

(Notes referred to by superior numbers may be found starting on page 169)

Contents

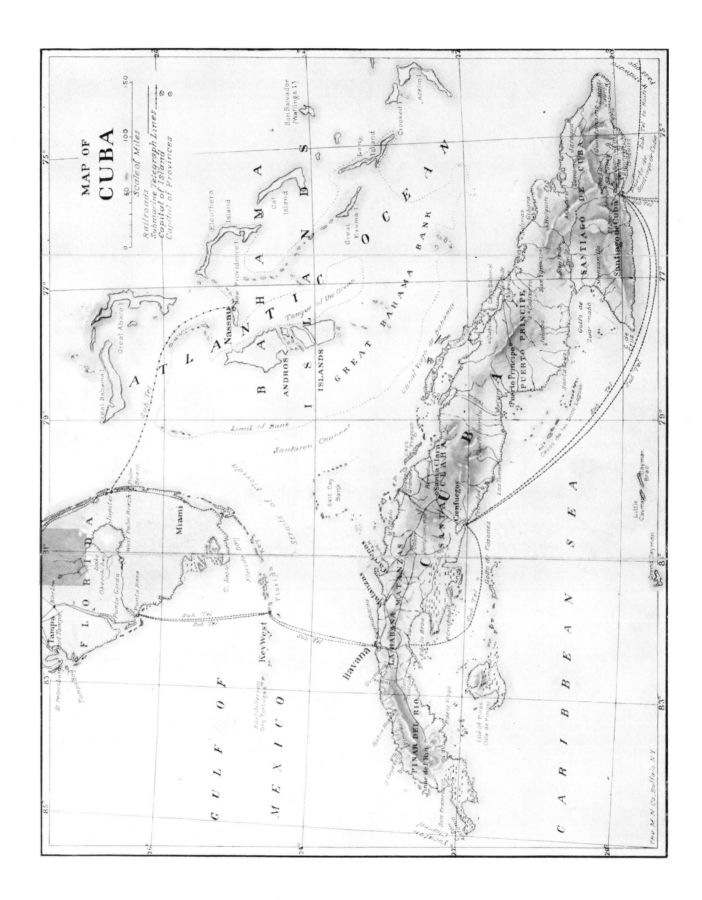

MAP OF
CUBA

Scale of Miles

Railroads
Submarine Telegraph Lines
Capital of Island
Capitol of Provinces

Preface

Few men or women born to this earth leave a legacy to be revered by future generations. Those few reach that stratum of achievement where fame never fades and their work is never forgotten.

Frederic Remington was one of these few. His star rises higher with the passing years. Admiration for and the value of the works he created increase constantly. The master portrayer of one of our country's most colorful eras, the vanishing of the Old West, his paintings, bronzes, and writings are authoritative and all show the touch of his genius.

My first visit to the St. Lawrence country is one that I will not forget. It was not so long ago that I cannot recall my meeting with a fine gentleman, Atwood Manley, who generously gave of his time to show me the places so closely related to Frederic Remington: the house and the room where he was born, the old county racetrack that was so much a part of the artist's early life, the Grass River where he went swimming as a boy, and the high hill overlooking Chippewa Bay where he spent his summers in later life.

Nor will I forget Mr. Manley's assistance in providing me with material which helped me in the preparation of this book. We can all be proud, those of us who love the work of Frederic Remington, of the little booklet that Mr. Manley wrote, "Frederic Remington in the Land of His Youth." In this important work the author gives to us the story of the artist's boyhood and the background that provided the foundation for his future brilliance.

Reflecting on his early life, it would seem to me that no single circumstance or series of events can be cited as the cause of Remington's development into one of America's greatest artists.

He was born and reared in a small country village of some fifteen hundred inhabitants. His mother and grandmother were plain, unassuming women. His grandfather, Seth Williston Remington, was a minister and one of the founders of what is now St. Lawrence University. His father was a newspaperman and ardent horseman. It might be assumed that from his father Remington acquired the ability to write so colorfully and to love and know horses so well that in later years his portrayals of them brought him his fame.

Frederic Remington instinctively loved everything military. This must have stemmed directly from his father. Just two months after Fred was born, October 1, 1861, Seth Pierre Remington was commissioned a Major in Scott's 900 or the Eleventh New York Cavalry. Frederic was four and a half when Colonel Remington returned home, a dashing officer and a true hero of the Civil War. The small boy could not help but worship this man and his noble deeds on the field of battle.

There is no evidence that young Frederic Remington had a particular talent for drawing. His early attempts show nothing more than the average experiments of many other youngsters. He was prolific, however, with his sketches of soldiers, both ancient and modern, covering the margins of his schoolbooks and notebooks with them. Even his letters were embellished with drawings of his first love, the soldier.

His first published drawing, made when he was an art student at Yale, appeared in the *Yale Courant* in 1879—a crude cartoon attempt, with no style or likeness to the work he was to do in future years.

His first published works as an illustrator for *Harper's Weekly* and *Outing Magazine* in the mid-1880s showed promise of what was to come. They, too, were crudely drawn, yet there was the first sign of talent.

It was by continuous hard work that this man, practically self-taught, began to develop his ability. A chronological survey of his work amazes one with its steady improvement. In just two short years after his first major attempt as a professional he was entrusted to do the illustrations for a series of articles that appeared in *Century Magazine* and that were eventually contained in a book, one of the finest to come out of that era, Theodore Roosevelt's *Ranch Life and the Hunting Trail*. From that time there could never be any doubt about his talent.

Frederic Remington had a natural inclination for action, tolerating nothing that lacked vitality. His natural gift, so important, was aptly described in a newspaper article published in 1893:

❦

He had a positive genius for facts. His eye caught with celerity and certainty of the shutter all the lens of the camera saw and much more besides. It took the recorded results of photographic experiment to verify Mr. Remington's own wonderful vision of the horse in action, a vision so instant and so comprehensive that the untrained observer was a long time in realizing that Mr. Remington was in what appeared to be unfamiliar action in the trotting and running horse.

❦

During the late 1880s and early 1890s Remington continuously followed the last days of action between cavalry and the Indian. Wherever the soldier laid his head one would be sure to find the artist, sketch pad in hand.

But the West that Frederic Remington had known and loved and painted and written about had all but vanished by the year 1895. The soldier and the Indian no longer confronted each other as in the old days. The Indian was relegated to the reservation and the soldier to the routine of post life. Remington, who had loved the military life, began to feel as listless as he believed the soldier felt. He pretty much settled down with his reminiscences. The stories that Owen Wister and Theodore Roosevelt were later to praise so highly began to roll from his pen, resulting in the famous *Pony Tracks*. There were the illustrations to accompany the stories. There was his first attempt at sculpture—the Bronco Buster—and others followed.

Comfortably settled in his home in New Rochelle, New York, he was interviewed one day and revealed his reflections:

❦

His dream is to follow a European campaign. With a soldier and a horse he can make a picture. With millions of soldiers and horses in the kaleidoscopic variety of a big war, its pomps and miseries, its glory and death, he can make no end of pictures that everybody will want to see.

❦

Clouds were hanging over an island to the south. The people of Cuba were thirsting for an independent way of life. They were completely tired of an oppression they had borne for centuries. The day would not be long in coming when that oppression would be challenged. Frederic Remington would be there to capture and record the history of the Spanish-American War as he had recorded those last years of the vanishing Old West.

DOUGLAS ALLEN

FREDERIC REMINGTON *and*
the Spanish-American War

A Thrilling Tale of Real Life In THE EVENING JOURNAL.

That Funny Page, That Sporting Page, That News Novelette, ALL (TO-MORROW) In THE EVENING JOURNAL.

NEW YORK JOURNAL

Copyright, 1897, by W. R. Hearst.

Tips on Sporting Matters THE BEST SPORTING PAGE in THE EVENING JOURNAL

FUN FOR ALL TO-MORROW In THE EVENING JOURNAL

NO. 5,176.   NEW YORK, SUNDAY, JANUARY 17, 1897.—52 PAGES.   PRICE FIVE CENTS.

RICHARD HARDING DAVIS AND FREDERIC REMINGTON IN CUBA FOR THE JOURNAL.

FREDERIC REMINGTON

RICHARD HARDING DAVIS

FREDERICK REMINGTON, the artist, and Richard Harding Davis, author and newspaper writer, have reached the insurgent army in the island of Cuba, where they go as representatives of the Journal. Mr. Remington is making sketches of the life and activity of the patriot army as he finds it, and Mr. Davis, acting as war correspondent, will have a new field of effort for his trenchant and brilliant pen.

Together they will present the true situation in the war-stricken island in more graphic and vivid style than it has yet been pictured to the American public.

Frederick Remington is beyond doubt the best known illustrator of military life alive to-day. Although a young man, Mr. Remington has won recognition rapidly by combining an early accumulated fund of experiences and a love for the unhackneyed phases of life with fine natural gifts as an artist and energy that seems exhaustless.

He is a native New Yorker, whose art education was begun in the Yale School of the Fine Arts and carried on at the Art Students' League of New York—that aggres-

sive American school which has turned out so many clever and original artists. About six years ago he went out among the cowboys of the West and found a wealth of material to work upon. The rough side of life on the plains appealed to him strongly, and he travelled through Wyoming, Kansas and Indian Territory, serving, meanwhile, in several Indian campaigns. All of his leisure moments were devoted to sketching. It was during this service that he gained such an intimate knowledge of the dress, appearance and habits of United States soldiers, cowboys, Indians, miners and frontier characters in general.

After going through an Indian war in Arizona he came East, but was soon sent back to join General Miles with a commission from Harper & Brothers. Since then he has been kept constantly busy drawing for the Harpers, the Century and some other magazines. The rush and swirl of his Indian ponies bring the breath of the prairies into his pictures. He fell in love with his work so completely that he once said that he wanted inscribed on his tomb when he

died: "This man knew the horse." He has been justly called the pictorial historian of the great West. He has covered every phase of that section's life from the North Saskatchewan to the Yaqui River, in Mexico, and has a rich fund of "notes" from these picturesque channels of experience. He and Mr. Davis have worked together before, and each is a valuable adjunct and inspiration to the other.

On the Cuban battle fields Mr. Remington will find a new background for his vivid sketch work, and the readers of the Journal are to have the benefit of his brilliant efforts there. He will give to scenes on the war-stricken island a life and touch of originality that will make them more real to the American people than anything in the shape of illustrations that has been offered since the beginning of the revolution.

Richard Harding Davis, the Journal's war correspondent with the insurgent army in Cuba, is almost too well known to the American public, both as an author and a newspaper man, to require introduction. His brilliant work for the Journal last year in describing, by cable, the ceremonies attending the

coronation of the Czar of Russia is still fresh in the minds of the readers of this paper.

Mr. Davis was educated at Lehigh and Johns Hopkins universities, with an especial view to a journalistic career. He chose to begin at the bottom, and took his first assignment as a reporter on one of the Philadelphia papers. After a long service in that city he came to New York. One year's work in newspaperdom here brought him an offer of the managing editorship of Harper's Weekly, which he accepted. His short stories won him a name in the literary world as an author of rarely entertaining style. "Gallagher and Other Stories," "Van Bibber and Others," "Princess Aline" and "Stories for Boys" have all attained a wide popularity.

As a descriptive writer, infusing every sentence with color and vigor, Mr. Davis occupies a secure position. He is young, but possesses a remarkably keen insight into human nature. The strength of his word pictures is remarkable, and his humor genuine and fine. Not only in America have his sketches and short stories been read with appreciation, but all Europe has acknowledged their merit.

1. Yellow Journalism

The Spanish-American War was short-lived but the events that led to it had a long history. The story of the war, as far as the area of this book is concerned, is the part Frederic Remington played in it. We might say that this story had its beginning in the latter part of the year 1895.

It was in September of that year that a young newspaperman, William Randolph Hearst, purchased the New York *Morning Journal*. This newspaper had a small circulation. Hearst was the type of man who thrived on challenge. His goal was to beat out the competition of other local papers, in particular, Pulitzer's *World*. Being a man who had a flair for the bold, splashing type of news and knowing what people liked to read, he set about meeting this competition.

Cuba at that time was in the throes of rebellion, and the stories that came out of the island could make good copy. Here was a people oppressed by a despotic government, and it was Hearst's theory that if the coverage was handled right he would have something of value to sell to the public. He began to treat the Cuban situation sensationally. His correspondents would report the struggle of a freedom-loving people against the tyranny of a cruel and powerful nation, for Spain at that time was a world power. Some of the reports were true and some had no foundation, but the headlines emblazoned in bold type and the dramatic treatment of events had the effect Hearst was striving for, and the New York *Journal* prospered. Staid, conservative newspapermen had a name for it— yellow journalism.

James Creelman, one of the *Journal*'s top reporters and a fine correspondent, had his own ideas on this terminology:

It has been said by those calm students of human events who were untroubled by

Murdering the Cuban Wounded

The Cuban Martyrdom

3

The Death of Rodriguez

the cries of oppressed Cuba that the war between the United States and Spain was the work of the "Yellow newspapers," that form of American journalistic energy which is not content merely to print a daily record of history, but seeks to take part in events as an active and sometimes decisive agent.

That was a saying of high reproach when the armed struggle began and when continental Europe frowned upon the American cause. "Yellow Journalism" was blood guilty. Its editors were enemies of society and its correspondents ministers of passion and disorder. Its lying clamours had aroused the credulous mob, overthrown the dignified policies of government, and dishonored international law.

But when the results of that conflict justified the instrumentalities which produced it, when the world accepts the emancipation of Cuba from the bloody rule of Spain as a glorious step in the progress of mankind, then the part played by the newspapers was forgotten and "yellow journalism" was left to sing its own praises, and its voice was long and loud and sometimes tiresome.[1]

The struggle in Cuba continued. Spain was forced to show her hand with sterner measures. General Don Valeriano Weyler y Nicolau was sent to the island. "The Butcher"—

A little man. An apparition of black—black eyes, black hair, black beard—dark, exceedingly dark complexion; a plain black attire, black shoes, black tie, and soiled standing collar and not a relief from the aspect of darkness anywhere on his person. "I care not for America, England—or anyone, but only for the treaties we have with them. They are the law. I know I am merciless, but mercy has no place in war. I care not what is said about me. I am not a politician. I am Weyler."[2]

It was in the issue of March 7, 1896, that *Harper's Weekly* published as its frontispiece, an illustration by Frederic Remington entitled, "The Flag of Cuba—Insurgent Cavalry Drawn Up for a Charge." This drawing was made from a photograph. Remington had not yet been to Cuba to draw on-the-spot occurences.

Later in the year, the rebellion continuing, General Weyler issued sterner measures. He attempted to strip the countryside of all means of support by moving the people to the towns and thus starve out the uprising. This did not produce the effects he desired but it did cause untold suffering to the people who died in great numbers for lack of food and from disease. The stories came through to the press.

The Flag of Cuba—Insurgent Cavalry Formed for a Charge

In December 1896, Remington was commissioned by the New York *Journal* to go to Cuba with Richard Harding Davis to illustrate and report on the struggle. Although the United States was not at war with Spain, the Spanish government was becoming cognizant of growing American interest in the events going on in Cuba and was not enthused by visits to the island by Americans. The Spanish navy blockaded Cuba to prevent, as much as possible, Cubans from fleeing the island and most certainly to prevent any arms and food from reaching the insurgents. Remington and Davis, notwithstanding, had made the decision, in good reporter style, to attempt running the blockade. Their stories could be of value to their paper only if they were eyewitness reports from the rebel side.

Previous arrangements had been made. They would leave Key West on the *Vamoose*, Davis describing it as "the fastest steam yacht made."[3]

On Christmas Day, 1896, Remington wrote to his wife, "*Vamoose* is here being painted gray—it is blowing hard and we may not go before to-morrow night."

It is known that the attempt was made before the end of the year, for on January 1, 1897, Davis wrote from Key West that, "We tried to cross fairly in the damn tub and it was her captain who put back."[4] The story is told that the *Vamoose* attempted a run three times but was unable to take the weather. In one of these attempts the two correspondents were having a hard time:

❧

Davis and Remington were lying in the scuppers and clinging to the shallow rail to keep from being washed overboard. The Chinaman cook, between lurches, was lashing together a door and some boxes to serve as a raft. Davis suggested to Remington the advisability of trying something of the kind for themselves.

"Lie still," Remington commanded, "you and I don't know how to do that. Let him make the raft. If we capsize I'll throttle him and take it from him." In a future discussion on the moral phase of such an action he remarked, "Why, Davis alone was worth a dozen sea-cooks. I don't have to talk of myself."[5]

❧

Hope of reaching the rebel forces via the *Vamoose* was abandoned. Remington wrote:

❧

Our patience gave out. The Spanish consul at Key West kept Weyler fully informed of our designs.

Mr. Davis proposed that, since we could not get in the coal-cellar window, we had best go around and knock at the front door. I should never have dreamed of such a thing, but Davis has the true newspaper impudence, so we arranged passage on the regular line steamer *Olivette* [later to enter the picture as the scene for one of the New York *Journal*'s sensational stories] for Havana.[6]

He wrote to Mrs. Remington from Key West:

It is now 4 o.c.—we leave at six—the boat is at the dock steaming up. The town is wild with excitement—we have only the custom house to fear. Two Cuban officers go with us—I am well—and I feel that I am to undertake quite the most eventful adventure of my life—I think there will be war with Spain.

Some years later Remington wrote an article for *Collier's Weekly* entitled "Under Which King?" in which he reminisced of the immediate events to come.

. . . Our passports were quaint little papers, made out on some sort of custom-house blanks by a friend in Key West, but plastered with gold seals and draped with ribbons like May queens.

Upon our arrival [in Havana], Consul-General Lee added us to his burden and escorted us up to the great Captain-General Weyler, who was at that time in the full glory of his "reconcentrado" and "forty-battalion" fame. To my simple democratic soul, the marble stairway of the palace which we entered looked like the Gates of Heaven. . . . There were gold-laced officers, black-robed church dignitaries, sentries and couriers coming and going or whispering by the way. They turned lupine eyes on us, but there was no resisting Lee. To be sure, his government was affording him no support. He represented no one but himself; but his doughty presence, and, I suppose, the foresight of the Spanish, as they thought of the American millions that were behind Lee when his day should come, made courtesy possible and imperative. After being introduced, General Lee sat on a sofa, which he filled with his impassive presence; Weyler teetered in a cane rocking-chair nervously; Davis squinted at the scene for future reference, and I made the only profile of Weyler on this side of the Atlantic on my cuff.

The interview was long, and we never flattered ourselves with having impressed Weyler with our innocence. No good ever came of the beautiful papers which he said would take us everywhere. We might as well have presented last-year's calendar to the Spanish officers. I saw ill-clad, ill-fed Spanish soldiers bring their dead and wounded

A Spanish Officer   Young Spanish Officer

General Weyler in the Field

into the city, dragging slowly along in ragged columns. I saw scarred Cubans with their arms bound stiffly behind them being marched to the cabañas. They were to face the black-line in the Laurel Ditch. I saw the "reconcentrados" being hurried in by the mounted guerillas, and the country was a pall of smoke from their burning homes.[7]

What Remington observed he drew and accompanied these illustrations with his written impressions and sent them off to the New York *Journal*.

In a letter dated January 15, 1897, Davis wrote to his mother from Matanzas, Cuba, that he had given Remington a note to mail to her in the States. In less than two weeks the artist-correspondent had become less than enamored of the whole thing. Completing what work he had started he sailed from Cuba and returned home but not before he is said to have sent a telegram to Hearst: EVERYTHING IS QUIET. THERE IS NO TROUBLE HERE. THERE WILL BE NO WAR. I WISH TO RETURN.

The terse reply came back. PLEASE REMAIN. YOU FURNISH THE PICTURES. I'LL FURNISH THE WAR.

On January 28 he wrote to his old friend Poultney Bigelow:

Just home from Cuba, saw more hell there than I ever read about. Went for New York *Journal*—small pox, typhoid, yellow jack, dishonesty, suffering beyond measure. Davis will tell and I will draw but can't do much in a Yellow Kid Journal—printing too bad.

On the water wagon for fair and working like mad man. You'll never help bury me, old hoss. I'm beating the game slowly surely—and only hope I will never be rich cause I don't think I would be any bloody common good if I had money.

My great aim in life is to take a Canadian canoe trip next fall. Going to get out a picture book this year.[8]

The picture book he referred to must well have been his *Drawings* which was published in that year of 1897.

Two weeks later, under the dateline February 12, 1897, one of the most controversial stories of yellow journalism appeared in the New York *Journal* and was accompanied by a Remington drawing. A dispatch had been received by the paper from Davis that the ship *Olivette*, American owned, had been boarded by Spanish police officers just prior to its return trip from Havana to the States. The story told of these officers searching suspected Cuban women, stripped of all clothing, for possible messages from the Cuban

(text continues on page 24)

Top: *Guerillas with Captured Pacificos*
Left: *An Officer of Spanish Guerillas*
Below: *A Spanish Guerilla*

SPANISH GUERILLAS BRINGING "PACIFICOS" INTO CAMP

GUINES, CUBA, *January 15, 1897.* The acts of the terrible savages, or irregular troops called "guerillas," employed by the Spaniards, pass all understanding by civilized man. The American Indian was never guilty of the monstrous crimes that they commit.

Their treatment of women is unspeakable, and as for the men captured by them alive, the blood curdles in my veins as I think of the atrocity, of the cruelty, practiced on these helpless victims.

My picture illustrates one case where the guerillas saw fit to bring their captives into the lines, trussed up at the elbows, after their fashion. *The New York* Journal, *January 24, 1897.*

SCOUTING PARTY OF SPANISH CAVALRY

HAVANA, CUBA, *January 17, 1897*. The appearance of the Spanish cavalry in the field is really pathetic. Fresh supplies of ponies, which are arriving daily from Texas, may occasionally lessen the extent of the misery somewhat, but for only a short time, for the hard usage which the poor brutes receive soon renders them pitiable objects.

These little ponies are in the last stages of exhaustion and disease, due to the hard work they are subjected to and the poor fodder they receive. The saddles used on these equine martyrs are of two kinds, and both are bad and cruel and torturing beyond description. The result is that nearly all the ponies have sore backs, some of which are past the stage where a veterinary's care or attention would do them any good, and this condition does not keep them from constant use.

The rough and insufficient nourishing power of the fodder of Cuba is almost useless for sustaining strength in the animals, and the men who bestride and urge them are totally indifferent to the comfort or care of the mounts—all of which is a long story. *The New York* Journal, *January 24, 1897.*

Top: *Scouting Party of Spanish Cavalry*
Right: *Regular Cavalryman—Spanish*

Top: *Spanish Troops in Action*
Left: *Insurgents Firing on a Spanish
    Fort "One Shot for a Hundred"*

16

SPANISH TROOPS IN ACTION

HAVANA, CUBA, *January 16, 1897.* The raw material of the Spanish army is good, but they have been demoralized, and their officer corps leaves much to be desired. They have a good rifle, carry 200 rounds of ammunition, and are good marchers, but they are defective in commissariat and rarely march over two days from their base. The insurgents "pot" into the head of their columns, whereat they halt, bunch up and rain badly aimed Mauser bullets. They form hollow squares when menaced by cavalry, and generally their tactics are obsolete, but in spite of this the enlisted men stand the "gaff" much better than they ought to be expected to considering their hollow leadership. *The New York* Journal, *January 31, 1897.*

ONE SHOT FOR A HUNDRED

HAVANA, CUBA, *January 16, 1897.* This is one of the favorite enterprises of the Cubans. They approach the little forts which fairly dot the landscape and fire a shot into it. Instantly a fusillade of Mausers reply, costing Spain, say five dollars, which in the aggregate foots up her heaviest bill. I heard a little fort in Jarves go off one night—bizz-z-z—and no answering shot. People rolled over in their bunks and went to sleep again. If the Cubans had only a few light field guns, the whole system of chicken-coop forts would go on the instant. *The New York* Journal, *January 31, 1897.*

SPANISH SOLDIERS RETURNING WITH WOUNDED COMRADES

HAVANA, CUBA, *January 16, 1897.* Nothing can be more pathetic than to see the little column of soldiers returning with their stricken comrades carried on stretchers with their blankets thrown over them. The half-starved people slouch along, dirty, ragged, with lack-lustre eyes and appeal to one's sympathies most powerfully. It is no wonder that some few desert and that they rob and forage unmercifully. When the boys are forced into the army to be maltreated as they are, there must be a powerful patriotism dwelling in them or they are highly deficient in enterprise. Northern troops mutiny under such conditions. *The New York* Journal, *January 31, 1897.*

Top: *Bringing in the Wounded*
Right: *Amateur Surgery in Cuba*

19

Spanish Cavalryman on a Texas Bronco

20

Fashions for Men!
Spring Designs from London and Paris in
Next Sunday's Journal.

NEW YORK JOURNAL

Copyright, 1897, by W. R. Hearst.

NO. 5,202. NEW YORK, FRIDAY, FEBRUARY 12, 1897.—14 PAGES. PRICE ONE CENT In Greater New York and Jersey City. | Elsewhere, TWO CENTS.

THE Yellow Kid in Ireland
Dat Blarney Stone is a Hollo Mokkery!
NEXT SUNDAY'S COLORED SUPPLEMENT.

LEXOW TO THE JOURNAL ON THE EVILS OF TRUSTS.

Head of the Legislative Investigating Committee Declares That Combinations of Capital for the Purpose of Crushing Out All Competition Cannot Be Defended Along Any Lines of Logic or Policy.

Albany, Feb. 11.

Editor New York Journal:

THE duty which devolves upon each member of the committee is a most solemn and difficult task, and one to be performed with reference to two paramount considerations—First, the welfare of the citizen, in its largest and most general sense; second, the welfare of the State, in the sense of its commercial prosperity and industrial progress.

These two propositions are closely interwoven and interdependent and a successful solution of the problems presented requires the consideration and application of both propositions. It is to be expected that, in the course of our labors, we shall have to meet the adverse criticism and hostility of interests which use the arguments of special pleading and sophistry to obscure the true issue. It is, therefore, the more important that the true facts shall be elicited, and that legislative action shall proceed prudently and conservatively along the lines of established conditions.

Nobody Favors the Existence of Trusts.

I conceive that nobody, except, perhaps, those financially interested, favors the existence of trusts, provided they disclose the characteristics inseparably connected with that kind of commercial entity popularly designated a "trust." That is to say, an aggregation of capital, the primary object of which is to obtain a monopoly, and whose every effort is directed toward the annihilation of competition, recognizing in every competitor an enemy to be crushed by such means as may accomplish that purpose most speedily and effectively. The objective point is the creation of absolute monopoly, involving the control of supply and distribution of product necessary to the welfare and convenience of the citizen.

It requires no argument to show that monopolies are not created over night, just as Rome was not built in a day. Progressive steps of years of development are necessary to evolve out of the sphere of free and equal competition the perfect flower of an absolute monopoly. Combinations of capital, call them by whatsoever name you please, are not in themselves objectionable; on the contrary, they appear to be the necessary logical evolution inseparable from the tendency of commercial development toward better conditions and higher civilization, involving greater facilities, more perfect product and lower prices to the consumer.

Wide Gulf Between Concentration and Monopoly.

Competition naturally leads to concentration, but there is a wide gulf and a long step between concentration and monopoly. The industrial and commercial prosperity of the Empire State should not be checked, nor any obstacle placed in the way of the largest possible expansion of enterprise in every field of human activity. But a phase of commercial development which checks individual effort, annihilates that full, free and fair competition which the law ordains, and leaves in its wake a trail of closed factories and ruined competitors, with labor on the one hand and consumer on the other, at the mercy of arbitrary decision as to volume of output and price of product, is one that cannot be defended along any lines of logic, policy or expedience.

I do not say that this exists. It would be highly improper for me to prejudice the question which is now under investigation. Both sides of this important question must be carefully and judiciously considered before any final conclusion is reached. Hasty or ill-advised criticism or action is to be deeply deplored. Every setp should be guarded with a single purpose—to obtain the greatest good for the largest number and subserve the greatest prosperity and progress of our State and city.

CLARENCE LEXOW,
State Senator.

SENATOR CLARENCE LEXOW.

CROKER FOR NEXT MAYOR?

John C. Sheehan Admits Tammany Leaders Are Considering Him.

He Declares, Moreover, That the Old Leader Will Run if the Wigwam Insists.

Citizens Offer the Civic Crown to Croker, but He Keeps Silence---Purroy Hails It as Sure Defeat.

If it is the judgment of Tammany that Mr. Croker should be the candidate for Mayor he will, I have no doubt, at the proper time declare his willingness to accept the nomination.—JOHN C. SHEEHAN.

AS a political sensation nothing more startling could be sprung than the announcement that Richard Croker may be Tammany's candidate for the first Mayor of Greater New York. That a considerable number of people in New York desire him to be Mayor is made certain by the fact that a delegation of citizens called upon him Wednesday and offered him the civic crown.

It is not a question of whether Mr. Croker is a candidate, but whether he will be made the Wigwam's candidate. Those who recollect the convention when Senator Hill, against his will, was made the Democratic nominee for Governor, know that the Tigers of Tammany do not consult personal wishes in the selection of a standard bearer. If they say to Mr. Croker, "You must be our nominee," the old leader must abandon the doctrine he established or else lead the fight. That Tammany may make the call is apparent from John C. Sheehan's statement that the leaders are considering Croker's name, and that if they conclude he should be the candidate he will be the candidate.

That is Tammany talk with the ring of the old days in the tone. It means that when they determine on a course they will proceed without conference or deal with other organizations.

A Fight of Comparisons.

The naming of Croker would be the signal to go in for a Tammany fight in a campaign of comparison between the administrations of Grant and Gilroy and that of Strong. It would be a call to the old Tammany, the tigers whose zeal has been dwarfed by inertia during the era of reform. There would be harmony in Fourteenth street again; peace brought about with the whip if not otherwise.

The Purroy rebellion, politicians think, would collapse. The bolting leader might keep up the pretence of a fight for a short time, but his followers would get under the Croker banner because they would

Continued on Third Page.

PURROY SAYS IT MEANS DEFEAT.

To the Editor of the New York Journal:

Time will show that the proposition to nominate Croker for Mayor of Greater New York is a mere joke and a petty trick. Nothing would be more satisfactory to opponents of Tammany as at present managed than for it to nominate any one of its prominent men, whose public career is really typical of its present or recent system or methods. Such a man would be defeated by an overwhelming majority, of which my friends and myself would qform a small part.

HENRY D. PURROY.

TO DEMAND WORK FOR THE POOR.

Moved by the Journal's Disclosures of Destitution Dr. Rainsford and Others Will Urge Mayor Strong to Push All City Contracts.

TERRIBLE DESTITUTION, SAYS DR. RAINSFORD.

I have been surprised to find a difference of opinion as to the actual poverty which exists. Some people and some of the newspapers try to convey the idea that there is no unusual poverty, while a large number of people and the rest of the newspapers say there is unusual distress at present. * * * I cannot conceive how any one can be blind to the terrible destitution which exists in many parts of New York City.

The Rev. Dr. Rainsford, Commander Booth-Tucker, of the Salvation Army; Ernest H. Crosby, of the Social Reform Club, and Moses Oppenheim comprise a committee which, actuated by the destitution existing in this city, as disclosed by the Journal, will endeavor to find work for the great army of the unemployed.

The committee will call on Comptroller Fitch early next week to ascertain what city work is to be done. It will then urge upon Mayor Strong and the heads of departments the crying necessity of immediately beginning the operations on the work, and thus give employment to thousands.

On Sunday the committee will visit the Central Labor Union and request the co-operation of that organization. Its building trades section has already taken favorable action in the matter.

Thus does the work of the Journal bear good fruit. It was the first to open the eyes of the community to the misery, poverty and distress of thousands where the charitable organizations could not or did not reach.

It was hard for many, whose paths do not lead them where this destitution is hidden from the world, to believe that men, women and children were starving each day. The Rev. Dr. Rainsford was not thoroughly convinced until he visited the Journal's relief station. There he saw the poorly clothed clamoring for food and fuel, and he went away to ponder.

Since then he has delved for facts. His wife has aided him. He now wonders "how any one can be blind to the destitution." His wife has learn how little children go to school to store their minds while their stomachs are empty.

Powerful Aids to Relief.

And now Dr. Rainsford has joined hands with Commander Booth-Tucker, Mr. Crosby, the College Settlement Association, the Social Reform Club and the Central Labor Union to open a vigorous campaign on behalf of the hosts of hungry and unemployed. They will put every agency that philanthrophy can suggest in operation to aid the poverty-stricken thousands. Im-

Continued on Fourth Page.

DOES OUR FLAG SHIELD WOMEN?

Indignities Practised by Spanish Officials on Board American Vessels.

Richard Harding Davis Describes Some Startling Phases of the Cuban Situation.

Refined Young Women Stripped and Searched by Brutal Spaniards While Under Our Flag on the Olivette.

By Richard Harding Davis.

TAMPA, Fla., Feb. 10.—On the boat which carried me from Cuba to Key West were three young girls who had been exiled for giving aid to the insurgents. The brother of one of them, Miss Clemencia Arango, is in command of the Cuban forces in the field near Havana. More than once the sister has joined him there and has seen fighting and carried back dispatches to the Junta in Havana. So for this she and two other young women, who were also suspected, were ordered to leave the island.

I happened to sit next to Miss Arango at table on the steamer. I found that she was not an Amazon, or a Joan of Arc, or a woman of the people, with a machete in one hand and a Cuban flag in the other. She was a well bred, well educated young person who spoke three languages and dressed as you see girls dress on Fifth avenue after church on Sunday. This is what the Spaniards did to these girls:

After ordering them to leave the island on a certain day, they sent detectives to their houses on the morning of that day and had them undressed and searched to discover if they were carrying letters to the Junta at Key West and Tampa. They then, an hour later, searched them at the Custom House as they were leaving for the steamer. They searched them thoroughly, even to the length of taking off their shoes and stockings, and fifteen minutes later, when the young ladies stood at last on the deck of an American vessel, with the American flag hanging from the stern, the Spanish officers followed them there and demanded that a cabin should be furnished them to which the girls might be taken, and they were then again undressed and searched for the third time.

Searched a Passenger on an American Ship.

Spanish officers, with red crosses for bravery on their chests and gold lace on their cuffs, strutted scowlingly about the deck while this was being done, and chancing to find a Cuban suspect among the passengers ordered him to be searched also, only they did not give him the privacy of a cabin, but stripped him of his clothes on the main deck of this American vessel before a gaping crowd of passengers and the skulking ship's captain and his crew.

In order to leave Havana it is first necessary to give notice of your wish to do so by sending your passport to the Captain-General, who looks up your record, and after twenty-four hours, if he is willing to let you go, vises your passport and so signifies that your request is granted. After you have com-

Remington's Imaginative Drawing

NEW YORK JOURNAL

Copyright, 1897, by W. R. Hearst.

NO. 5,203.

NEW YORK, SATURDAY, FEBRUARY 13, 1897.—12 PAGES.

PRICE ONE CENT In Greater New York | Elsewhere and Jersey City. | TWO CENTS

MINISTER DE LOME'S RETORT

He Says Spain Has a Perfect Right to Search an American Vessel.

Washington, Feb. 12.---Senor Dupuy de Lome, the Spanish Minister, to-night made the following statement to the Journal regarding Richard Harding Davis's story of the searching of women on the Olivette at Havana:

"I don't care to comment on a newspaper story; for I don't believe a word they say.

"The Spanish authorities have a perfect right to board an American steamer, or any other kind of a vessel, and search persons, be they men or women, whom they suspect. A request to the steamer officials is not necessary.

"The government officers have the authority to make the search without first getting the captain's consent."

[De Lome evidently bases the Spanish position on two things: First. An American vessel, or the vessel of any nation, is absolutely under the control of the Spanish Government as to rights of search so long as she is in Spanish waters. Second. Under the treaty of 1795 Spain is given the right to search American vessels, even on the high seas, for contraband of war.]

[The outrage consists, in the opinion of experts, more in the manner of the search than in the fact. These searches are no new story. They have been going on ever since the insurrection broke out.

In the case of the Olivette, the Spanish exercised a right which, however outrageous in manner, is technically unassailable in international law.]

Senor Dupuy De Lome, Minister of Spain at Washington.

AROUSED BY SPAIN'S ACT.

Congress Will Hear To-day of the Search Outrage on the Olivette.

LAW MAKERS INDIGNANT.

Richard Harding Davis's Story of Inhumanity to Cuban Girls Brings Forth Strong Words.

STATE DEPARTMENT HAS NO REPORT YET.

Washington, Feb. 12.—The story told by Richard Harding Davis of the outrageous search in which Cuban girls were searched aboard the American steamer Olivette has aroused so much indignation here that a resolution on the matter will be offered in the House to-morrow. The fact will be urged that, while Spain technically has the right to search vessels in her ports, this in no way excuses the disgraceful conduct of the officials at Havana.

State Department Stirred.

The Olivette search was the chief topic of State. It was generally agreed that such incidents afford the best opportunity this Government could have of making demands upon Spain and give the best excuse for abandoning the attitude of patience and toleration toward Madrid with regard to Cuba.

The Navy Department officials refrain from expressing themselves regarding the necessity for a warship at Havana. They say that the appearance of one vessel there would call for the entire fleet. Its ominous aspect would not be dispelled by...

SENATOR WILSON WOULD ANNEX CUBA.

Washington, Feb. 12.

Editor New York Journal:

The outrageous search of those two Cuban women should be investigated at once by the State Department. An indemnity should also be demanded. The American flag should protect all passengers on an American ship.

I am an annexationist, boldly and above board. I would have Cuba if I could. In fact, I think we should annex in some way or other all the countries on this hemisphere. Go up even and take Greenland, with all her ice. Send the other fellows back across the water where they belong. War is a terrible thing, but I do not know but it is a good thing. All the territory we have acquired has come through war in some shape or other, and the Republic has broadened and strengthened. I would purchase when we could, but I would get hold of all the islands owned by European powers some way or other.

I think a warship should have been sent to Havana at the outbreak of the insurrection, not to intimidate, but to guard, American interests. We need one there now, and should have it. Such an outrage as this should not pass unnoticed or unpunished. We will hear of trouble with Spain yet.

JOHN L. WILSON,
United States Senator from Washington.

comment in the State and Navy departments to-day. At the State Department no official report furnishes an account of such, nor does, say the authorities, prompt action would be made to Madrid. An action from Consul General Lee or the diplomatic representatives in Cuba disrespect for the American flag and ill-treatment of women would have been subject of common decency would have for an investigation of such occur...

...tement which Mr. Davis makes the of his despatch from Tampa and to stir the State Department from their leniency and to earlier...

them to break the studied mystery or silence with which they surround affairs the excuse that the cruiser came to the Cuban port for the mere purpose of exercising regard for the American flag or of protecting helpless women on board American ships when their cringing captains are inhumanly powerless.

State Department in Ignorance.

The trouble appears to be that such instances as that in the cable of the Olivette either do not reach the Consul-General or he has not yet reported the incident to the State Department. The Washington...

Continued on Second Page.

ROUGH SEAS INTERFERE.

Fleet at Charleston Prevented from Going Through the Manoeuvres—The Indiana Arrives.

Charleston, S. C., Feb. 12.—Nothing has been done so far in the way of the naval manoeuvres and the sea is running so strong outside that the gun practice of the ships is interfered with.

This afternoon the cruiser Marblehead came up in the city and anchored off the battery. She has received orders to proceed to Jacksonville Monday, and it is understood that she will go from there to Mobile in a few days. The Vesuvius is anchored near the rest of the vessels, and gave no intimation of an attempt to run the blockade. The Dolphin, which in fact, was apparently having an uncomfortable time of it in the heavy sea that was running. She was rolling and plunging about in a manner that rendered a footing on her deck insecure to landsmen. The Amphitrite was coaled during the day, but she will not rejoin the fleet until to-morrow.

STANTONS TO BE ARRESTED.

Alleged Kidnappers of Millionaire Richardson in England.

Montreal, Feb. 12.—It is learned here that the Stantons, man and wife, who are said to have kidnapped the United States millionaire, Richardson, are under surveillance in England, and that they will be arrested as soon as the necessary papers are obtained.

The outrage consists, in the opinion...

DEPEW MAY NOW PACK HIS TRUNK.

Morton Clears the Way for Him to Be Ambassador to England.

ORGANIZATION FOR HIM.

Platt, Odell, Hackett and Lauterbach Express Their Wishes to McKinley.

Dr. Chauncey M. Depew will in all human probability be the next Ambassador to England, and thus a positive statement made by the Journal on February 1 is corroborated. The only obstacle that really ever stood in his way was the candidacy of ex-Governor Morton, and now that gentleman has immeasurably simplified the situation by withdrawing his name from consideration. He did so in a letter carried to Canton by Charles T. Saxton, in which he not only told Major...

Continued on Second Page.

LONDON PAPERS DISCUSS THE BALL.

Bradley Martin Affair Eulogized in the Cabled Reports.

"PERFECT," SAYS THE TIMES

New York Society Men and Women Seen at Their Best.

(Copyright, 1897, by W. R. Hearst.)

London, Feb. 12.—English and French papers to-day are full of accounts of the Bradley Martin ball, reviewing, for the most part, the spectacular side of the function. There is here, of course, a tendency to poke a certain amount of fun at this gorgeous display of magnificence, and the evocation of monarchical memories in up-to-date...

Continued on Second Page.

PULLMAN COMES TO STOP HIS SON.

Chicago Millionaire Does Not Approve of the Wine Business.

ESCAPADE IN CHICAGO.

It Is Said Young Pullman Was Disinherited as a Matter of Discipline.

Chicago, Feb. 12.—Last night when George M. Pullman, the palace car magnate, opened his New York Journal and read that his son, Sanger, was going into the business of selling champagne, he was so deeply affected that this afternoon he departed for New York with the express intention of dissuading his disgraced heir from such a purpose and, if possible, effecting a reconciliation with him. His friends say he was more markedly agitated than at any time during the great Debs strike, when his millions were at stake.

It was less than a month ago that Sanger was disinherited and told to go out in the cold world and shift for himself. How he went to New York and became engaged by Frank Hubbard as an agent for the sale of a certain brand of champagne has been told in the Journal.

Sanger is one of a pair of twins. George M. Pullman, Jr., being the other. They were born twenty-two years ago and had so much alike that their intimate friends have trouble in telling them apart. They were hardly one of kniferbockers when they set a pace in life as swift as to astonish their older and better seasoned companions. They were furnished with plenty of money and the liberal to indulge in any fancy that came up to them naturally...

His Brother Settled Down.

Still, he was greatly reflected a year ago when George M., Jr., became engaged to Miss Felicite Oglesby, the daughter of ex-Governor Oglesby, and, in order to satisfy that young lady dropped his objectionable habits. The young fellow was devotedly attached to his fiancee and soon settled down to a quiet life. Pullman pere fondly hoped that the eventual example set by one son would be followed by the other, but he was disappointed.

Sanger showed no signs of slacking his pace, and then and rise again Mr. Pullman found it necessary to bring all his influence to bear to save the youth from trouble, but the latter was so hardly out of one scrape before he ran into another. These "auction pranks" had a culmination a few weeks ago, when Sanger appeared at the Auditorium Annex in company with a woman whose reputation was not of the best and introduced her as his wife.

Summoning the boy before him, Mr. Pullman asked for an explanation; none was forthcoming, and Sanger was informed that he was disinherited... Mr. Pullman mandate and make his own way in the world. If he conducted himself properly he would again be welcomed to the Pullman hearthstone; but if he did so he need not look for a penny of the Pullman millions. Sanger never whimpered, but swallowed his medicine like a man, and, as has been proved, he lost no time in putting himself in the way of making a living.

Does Not Approve of Selling Wine.

It is a question which scandalized Mr. Pullman the more—the son Auditorium episode, or the fact that the son had determined to make his way by selling wine. The life of a wine agent is not an easy one, and he is taken to places in the pursuit of business that are not esteemed by careful fathers...

Preparing to Meet His Father.

Sanger Pullman and evidently heard of his father's visit last evening, for at 7 o'clock he retired to his apartment at the Northumberland Hotel, presumably to prepare for the ordeal. He told word that under no circumstances should he be disturbed.

A FOOT OF SNOW; MANY BLOCKADES.

Yesterday's Big Storm Congested Traffic Everywhere.

WORK FOR THE STARVING

Unemployed to the Number of 6,500 Were Put at Shovelling Snow.

BLOCKADE IN PARK ROW.

Sweeping Machine Broke Down and Delayed Cars Till Its Removal Was Effected.

ELEVATED ROADS, TOO, SUFFERED.

On the Sixth and Third Avenue Lines Men Were Stationed Between Stations to Signal the Condition of the Tracks.

STATISTICS OF THE SNOW STORM.

Depth of snow, in inches.	12
Blockades	...
Vessels delayed	...
Trains behind time	...
Snow shovellers employed	6,500
Accidents	79

Snow began falling at 3.30 o'clock yesterday morning. It fell steadily all day and far into the night, until it lay a foot deep in level places. Then the snow changed to sleet and back again to plain, beautiful snow. It impeded traffic in many streets in the city, particularly in those running to the ferries. This was especially true of Ivey, Cortlandt, Fulton and Whitehall streets, the each one of those streets most of the blockades came moreover occurred, although Chambers street, Park row, Desbrosses and West streets had their share of this kind of trouble.

Even on the elevated roads there was slight delay in running the trains. This was because the heavy fall of snow obscured the tracks, and engineers had to slow up and proceed cautiously. On the Sixth and Third Avenue lines men were placed between the stations to signal the engineers whether or not the track was clear.

Although the offices of the Street Cleaning Department were closed, it being a legal holiday, Deputy Commissioner Gibson was on hand attending to special business in connection with the storm. At noon he had a large force of men at work, shovelling snow from the streets into wagons. The first big snow storm of the season, he said, cost the department about $185,000. The last one cost $185,000, making a total of $340,000. He couldn't say definitely, but thought all of the money included in the original appropriation and in the two or three transferred since made to the account for the removal of snow had been exhausted. He expressed the belief, however, that there would be no trouble in securing a further transfer of money to meet the expenses incidental to the removal of snow.

At the headquarters of Contractor C. W. Farman it was learned that within two hours fifteen hundred men had been engaged and put to work at clearing the streets. No considerable difficulty was experienced in securing carts, but four-odars-5 o'clock some thousand of them were in operation.

Fragmentation Pains said that the storm was general in scope and even extended out to sea. The boat, in his opinion, would, however, run to rain by this sweep...

HACKENSACK STILL FAST.

The Ferryboat Stuck on the Sunken Meadows and Cannot Be Moved.

The Hackensack, the double decked ferryboat of the New York & College Point Ferry Company, went hard aground at Sunken Meadows in the Sound, yesterday in the midst of a blinding snowstorm. There were nine passengers and several teams on board, and they were brought in shore by tugs and a lighter.

The Hackensack was due to leave College Point on her first trip to the city at 6 o'clock in the morning. As a rule the passengers are farmers with loads of produce for the city markets, and merchants anxious to get to work. Yesterday being a holiday there were but half a dozen teams, with their drivers, and four other passengers. The storm was so severe that...

Chauncey M. Depew, Our Probable Envoy to England.

rebels. We point out that Remington was home at the time and therefore could only assume that the story was true and in consequence drafted the picture as he visualized it.

The rival newspaper *World* exposed the story as unfounded and forced the New York *Journal* to retract. Mr. Davis's version was published and read as follows in part: "For the benefit of people with unruly imaginations, of whom there seem to be a larger proportion in this country than I had supposed, I will state again that the search of these women was conducted by women and not by men, as I was reported to have said, and as I did not say in my original report of the incident."

The Remingtons spent the summer of 1897 at Cranberry Lake in the Adirondack Mountains. It was a favorite spot of the artist, who had whiled away many a leisure hour there occupied in hunting, fishing, and canoeing.

United States relations with Spain ran hot and cold. Weyler was dismissed from his post and a more lenient attitude in Spanish government toward the Cuban situation was in prospect. All erupted, however, with the news of the blowing up of the battleship *Maine* in Havana harbor. The brink had been reached. The date, February 15, 1898.

Mr. Augustus Thomas, close friend of the Remingtons, narrates the story:

One morning in February, James Waterbury, the agent of the Western Union Company in New Rochelle, telephoned me that the *Maine* had been blown up and sunk in the harbor of Havana. Knowing the interest the report would have for Remington, I immediately called him on the telephone and repeated the information. His only thanks or comment was to shout "Ring off!" In process of doing so I could hear him calling the private telephone number of his publishers in New York. In his mind his campaign was already actively under way.[9]

Some of this campaign may have had more serious aspects for Remington, for in the diary of Miss Emma L. Caten, sister of Eva Remington, there is written the entry under the date of February 17, 1898, "Eva and Fred are in Washington to-night."

A further entry in the diary dated March 14, 1898: "I am waiting further communication relative to the movements of F. Remington. I do not want war or its fearful results but I would like to have Fred 'do' the forts."

The situation was taking on serious proportions. Our East Coast defenses were of the utmost importance, for, if war were in the offing, a strike by the enemy on this vital area could not be ignored.

A First Lesson in the Art of War—Recruits for the Two Additional Artillery
Regiments at Fort Slocum, Davids Island, Long Island Sound

Major-General Nelson A. Miles, U.S.A., Inspecting the Defences of New York

27

Fred did "do" the forts. On March 26, 1898, *Harper's Weekly* published his drawing "A First Lesson in the Art of War—Recruits for the Two Additional Regiments at Fort Slocum, Davids Island, Long Island Sound." In the April 2 issue of the same magazine there appeared "Major-General Nelson A. Miles, U.S.A., Inspecting the Defenses of New York." This same issue carried a narrative by Remington entitled "The Training of Cavalry," a treatise on that very important phase in the education of an aspiring cavalryman. In that era the cavalry was a vital arm of our fighting force in the event of war.

2. The Training of Cavalry[1]*

It was two years since I had visited the cavalry post at Fort Meyer, Virginia. At that time I had supposed that our new system of horse-training and Cossack riding had reached the limitations of man and beast. But upon again seeing the drill I was amazed to find that there are seemingly no bounds to this thing. The horses seemed to use their brains almost as much as the riders used theirs, while in no circus which it has been my fortune to see has the rider equalled what all United States troops could do at that post.

I fear almost to tell about it. I should not expect to be believed had not many thousands of delighted people witnessed the same feats by some of the same troopers at the military and athletic tournaments held at the Madison Square Garden in New York.

In the first place, Colonel Sumner, commanding the Sixth Cavalry, said distinctly it was his policy not to permit anything like competition, as it would tend to the extra training of a few men at the expense of the others, and to its attendant jealousy or laxity. Consequently cooks, extra-duty men, and all other enlisted men at Fort Meyer could do everything which one saw in the riding-hall. Every soldier was of necessity an athlete in training; he could not be otherwise. They were all Americans—a very high grade of young fellows—all good material for noncommissioned officers, and some for even higher honors if war should summon their energies. They were each and every one finished horsemen, as well as daring riders, not only practically but theoretically.

Lieutenant Short of Troop A was good enough to initiate me into the opening secrets by taking two freshly arrived "remounts," not previously ridden or handled, to the riding-hall. Here he put on his "hackamore" in lieu of a bridle, and by a simple system of ropes running from broad straps around the pasterns to rings at the bottom of a broad leather surcingle he began. He slowly brought the horse to its knees, saying, "lie-down-down-down." The horse fought, but not very hard, because Mr. Short was so patient and gentle with it. He sought not to excite or anger the animal. He would have taken all day if necessary, but after ten minutes the horse succumbed to the inevitable and lay down. It was petted and allowed to rise, then the other one was handled similarly. Then the horses came to recognize that man was their master, and that they had nothing to fear from him.

*Remington's own account.

Hurdling on Three Horses, United States Regular Cavalry

A Model Squadron—Over the Hurdles in Line

The Training of United States Cavalry—A Roman Race at the Riding-Hall, Fort Myer, Virginia

33

These being particularly tractable beasts, Mr. Short said he would carry their training farther at that time, in my interest, although it was not the custom to do so, for fear of overdoing matters. He threw a horse, and upon its recovering its feet, mounted it bareback. The horse was dazed, and did not apparently mind this new indignity. It was then put through the "bending" movements by the easy leg pressure, to which it lent ready obedience. Then it was led up to a low brush hurdle at the end of a chute, and following a veteran troop-horse, was forced over the hurdle on a "lunge." After their first lesson these two horses were better broken than half the mounts one sees in the parks. All that remained was wrought out by patience, and never by any possibility was a horse hurt or maddened by too great a call on its energies. When the horse was issued to a soldier the man took it to the riding-hall in his leisure moments and put it carefully through its schooling. If a horse by over-training became resentful it was let out of school for the day—for all the world like a sulky boy. They did not rub an education into it.

As to the trooper, he was gone at in much the same way. It was found at long intervals that some men were too clumsy or timid for horse-soldiers, and they went elsewhere. But by proceeding gently, by a vigorous training of the muscles, the soldier gains confidence in himself. At the end of a time, which varies greatly in men, he will attempt absolutely anything with a horse, and he has so much activity, so much knowledge of how to fall, so much "horse *sabe*," that he is seldom hurt as he sprawls in the soft tan-bark of the ring.

Four troops were successively drilled in the hall before an admiring audience—the first two in intricate music-rides, side passages in line, lying down, manoeuvers calculated to show their perfect training.

The third troop, drilled by Lieutenant Nissen, came in bareback—and there is where I am afraid of my statements; I should not have believed it if I had not seen it. One should be or have been a bit of a horseman himself fully to appreciate such a thing. I have attempted to show in my drawings some of the most astonishing feats; and, mind you, these were performed by every horse and man on the tan-bark. The hurdle jumping was done by men of Lieutenant Short's troop while standing up in the saddle with their course shoes on. This, I am told, is more difficult than when they are bareback with rubber-soled tennis shoes.

The Roman race was indulged in by three men at a time, each controlling three horses bareback. They were in a large riding-hall, and not in a circus ring, and the horses were run at top speed, so fast, indeed, that two of them were upset on the turns.

A Limber in Action

There was much beside this—notably a soldier running beside three linked horses, vaulting while at the hurdle jump clean over two mounts to land on the nigh horse. Also, when mounted double, and at full career, the men changed places in a most astonishing way, the front rider whirling with his back to the rear man while supported by his heel on the rear rider's toe.

It is exceedingly gratifying to know that our cavalry soldiers play their games so well. For myself, I have never seen any class of rider in any part of the world who could do as well or anything like as well—a large part of the "flash" riding of Cossacks and Comanche Indians being done by artificial aids of either saddlery or loops of various sorts which support them.

I wish those blatant patriots who are so ready to rely on our 10,000,000 able-bodied but untrained "available" men in the event of war could go and look these cavalry men over, and ask themselves how long it will take to qualify the proper proportion of this material for troopers for the Sixth Cavalry.

3. Seagoing Plainsman

In a letter to Remington dated December 28, 1897, Teddy Roosevelt, then Assistant Secretary of the Navy, called him a "seagoing plainsman." This undoubtedly refers to the artist's attempt to get to Cuba with Richard Harding Davis. Roosevelt and Remington corresponded frequently over the years, and there was little that the future President didn't know about the comings and goings of his friend.

On April 20, 1898, Miss Emma Caten, who was visiting her sister, Eva Remington, in New Rochelle, New York, inscribed in her diary:

I have been here a week and not a word in my diary. The war excitement has every other thing out of mind. The "Iowa" seems to have our closest attention for that is the one Fred R. is on and although we expect it to ride safely through the storm, still, we cannot but feel anxious until it is all over.

Remington always kept his wife posted as to his whereabouts, and we can assume that the date of this entry by his sister-in-law was the result of a letter just received. It was not until the 22nd that official orders were given to blockade Cuba, the *Iowa* being a participant in this action.

In the following two articles, one, untitled, appearing in the book *Cuba at a Glance* and the other "Wigwags from the Blockade" appearing in *Harper's Weekly*, May 14, 1898, Remington portrays this event—his "landing" on the battleship and his impressions of his seven days at sea.

From Cuba at a Glance

I boarded the tug which took all the shore leave men off to their ships and was "landed" on the *Iowa*—battleship—an iron island floating on the sea.

The Captain was the celebrated Fighting Bob Evans of common report, but aboard

NIGHT SPECIAL.

AN AMERICAN PAPER FOR THE AMERICAN PEOPLE
NEW YORK JOURNAL

NIGHT SPECIAL.

NO. 5,618—P. M.
NEW YORK, MONDAY, APRIL 4, 1898.
PRICE ONE CENT.

BOTH HOUSES,
IN UPROAR, THREATENING REVOLT,
WARN M'KINLEY.

Arraignment of President Cheered in Senate and House.

Washington, April 4.—The Senate is for war. It is for making the Maine the vital issue in the controversy with Spain. If there is not radical action declaring the blowing up of the United States battle ship in itself an act of war, entailing all the consequences of such an act, every indication points to action which will bring matters to a head at once.

The Senate is determined to compel Spain to make reparation for the destruction of the Maine or to lose its hold in Cuba.

Through the speeches to-day of Senator Perkins, of California; Senator Mantle, of Montana, and Senator Clay, of Georgia, warning was given the President that the Senate does not intend he shall minimize the loss of the Maine and the massacre of her crew. Convinced that Spain is officially responsible, they want to hold her responsible.

Senator Perkins stated the case for the Senate when he said:

"Men do not arbitrate questions of honor; neither do nations. The destruction of the Maine is beyond the pale of arbitration.

"Gold will not atone for blood."

URGED DECLARATION OF WAR AT ONCE.

Senator Rawlins, of Utah, who wants to declare war against Spain, urged Congress to act at once. Congress should not wait upon the President, he argued, but should take the responsibility and act to-day.

He said the Committee on Foreign Relations was satisfied what action ought to be taken, and that he had been informed the Executive had requested the committee not to take that action which it had decided upon.

Forty-eight days had gone by since the destruction of the Maine by Spaniards, he said, and yet no action had been taken. Now the time had come to act.

In the House the same spirit reigned which reigned in the Senate. After

Continued on Fourth Page.

TEXAS SAILS STRIPPED FOR ACTION.

Suddenly Ordered to Leave at Once, with Decks Cleared.

Orders were received late this afternoon by the battle ship Texas, lying in the Brooklyn Navy Yard, to get to sea at once and join the Flying Squadron at Hampton Roads.

The battle ship will sail at the first flood tide.

The orders further directed that she sail with her decks cleared for action.

Much surprise was caused among the officers of the ship and at the yard at this sudden change of plans. It had been intended to hold the Texas to convoy the new cruisers San Francisco and Albany.

As soon as the sailing orders were received the deck and quarters were stripped of wood. The superfluous articles had all been tagged with pieces of brass on which the word "overboard" was stamped. Whenever fighting orders are received these articles will be thrown over.

The chests of the marines and men-of-warsmen were stowed away below.

Spain Accepts Pope's Mediation; Says McKinley Planned It.

Washington, April 4.—The one distinct fact that comes out of all the rumors, assertions and denials concerning the alleged intervention of the Pope in the issue between Spain and the United States, is that Spain is clearly trying to create the impression that there is to be such intervention and that it comes at the instigation of the United States.

On this last point an official denial has been issued from the White House. But even that denial is not satisfactory; it reads that the American Government has not "cabled" a request to the Pope to use his good offices for peace.

On the other hand the Spanish Minister in London has positively asserted that the United States did ask the Pope to intervene, that the Pope consented, and that Spain saw no reason for objection.

DENIAL BY MARTINELLI.

Here again comes Mgr. Martinelli, the Apostolic Delegate in Washington, with an absolute denial that the Pope has offered to mediate.

"The Holy Father never offers his good offices in disputes," explained Dr. Rooker, Secretary of the Delegate, and speaking for Mgr. Martinelli. "In order for him even to consider such a proposition, it would be necessary for both Governments concerned to make a formal request for such good offices.

"This request would have to come through the recognized channels of diplomacy—that is, the Secretary of State in each nation would write this request to the Papal Secretary of State, and not until the Papal Secretary had formally announced the Pope's willingness to act in such a capacity could it be announced as in the Madrid dispatch this morning. The United States has made no such request."

It was further explained by the Delegate that the presence of Archbish-

Continued on Second Page.

EXTRA
NO 14
LATEST NEWS
BOND SYNDICATE WORKING FOR AN ARMISTICE

WASHINGTON, April 4.—Efforts are being made by the McCook bond guarantee syndicate to arrange an armistice between the Cubans and Spain. The Cuban insurgent government has stipulated that it will not agree unless the terms provide for the recognition of Cuban independence. Colonel McCook is in Washington to-day.

YOUNG WOMAN NABS A DIAMOND THIEF.

BOSTON, April 4.—Miss Kittie M. Burke at noon to-day captured a diamond thief named William Ross, who was running away with a tray of gems from the jewelry store of John L. Graves at No. 33 Beacon street. The prisoner looks like a minister, and when searched $310 in bills were found in his pockets.

SUICIDE IN WASHINGTON HOTEL.

WASHINGTON, April 4.—William P. Herbert, of Virginia, committed suicide at his hotel by cutting his throat. He left a note saying he was tired of life. Herbert has a son, Edmund, at the Boston Technical Institute, and another named Beverly, studying law at Columbia, S. C.

POWERS TO SAVE SPAIN FROM WAR AT HOME.

Washington, April 4.—Spain, goaded to desperation by a two-fanged with a knowledge of the hopelessness of conflict with the United States, and of the insurrection that will doubtless follow a concession to the demands of this country—has, it is stated, found a loophole through which to escape war.

The authority for this statement is a diplomat, high in the service of his country, who, for obvious reasons, has declined to permit the use of his name in connection with the disclosure.

"The plan," he said, "by which Spain hopes, as a last resort, to evade the inevitable disaster to her of war with the United States is, practically, by a concession to the demands of the American nation.

"While the Spanish Government has been loudly crying that its honor and the integrity of its dynasty would not permit a single backward step, Spain was known throughout Europe for a mode of escape, for something which would permit a retreat from her vainglorious stand and not arouse the ire of her people.

GUARANTEE AGAINST REVOLUTION.

"In vain did Spain plead with the European powers—with France, Germany, Austria in turn—to countenance her attitude toward the United States, and lend their moral support, if not their armed aid.

"But these powers were not to be drawn into the matter in either of the ways. They had to consider the other nations of Europe as well as Spain, and were deterred by matters at their own thresholds.

"Now, however, France, Germany and Austria have come forward in a surprising manner. Although they had refused to stand in any active and visible opposition to the United States, they pledge themselves to uphold Spain in the event of insurrection following an abandonment of her position.

"This gives to Spain the needed loophole. She can now for the first time consider with equanimity the possibility of avoiding a clash with the United States and of preserving her dynasty, for civil war would set the throne trembling.

"Thus Spain is ready to hoodwink her people and escape from a conflict she now will prove to be so unequal.

"The Carlists and Weylerites are now ready, she knows, to arise against the throne if it gives the slightest indication of yielding to this country. With the most severe, she wishes to be spared the horrors and dangers of civil war.

Wild Applause in the House Galleries at Representative Bailey's Fierce Thrust at McKinley.

A tremendous storm of applause broke out in the galleries and floor of the House to-day when Representative Bailey, Democratic leader of the House, voiced the disgust of his party and the country at the delay policy of the Administration. Here is the scene sketched by Artist Williams at Washington that caused Speaker Reed to vigorously pound his gavel while Mr. Bailey retorted:

"These galleries are but a miniature of the people. What you hear here can be heard over the country."

ship I found him a calm-eyed man—very plain and straightforward in his affairs. It was Captain Evans simply—and stand up when you say it and have your statement straight, for the weather roll in the Captain's eye as it turns over your person is very severe and not encouraging.

To a shore man the environment of a modern battleship is more strange than a dream. It cock-tails up in your mind with a nut and bolt factory as a base—but the other mixtures are like an international exhibition, a World's Fair of people and things. The throb of engines—the shrill squealing of bo'suns' whistles—electric lights—cranes swinging coal in from the lighter "longside," long guns bigger than forest trees sticking everywhere, sharp orders, gentlemanly officers in white duck trousers, and bare-footed jackies running about, monkey-like in their movements, while marine guards strut martially across the deck.

You go to the dining-room—or, as they say, "ward-room"—through another room which makes you chilly because it is filled with long fish-like torpedoes which are loaded with dynamite or other nervous things which are difficult to tolerate on intimate living terms.

And to-morrow we are going to war. One doesn't in these days go to war often enough to make it commonplace, and yet strain as I would, hunt high and low, officers and sailormen, I could find nothing but the most deadly apathy concerning the whole proceeding. I don't think it was because they were overused to going to war, but they have eaten and slept and drilled and thought so much within this ship's sides that it has eaten up their other thoughts. They are a part of the big machine, the *Iowa*, and she was built to go to war—so why not?

Every one was happy on the fine morning, going to war. Sailors hate a blockade—they dread inaction. They want to mix it up with the batteries, but the blessed old United States Army is not ready yet, so they must wait; but they took it out on the soldiers, and dearly I wish for some of them to be along to take their own part—for it's no funeral of mine if the tents, the grub, the mules and the guns are not there ready for men to use.

"To-morrow may bring great things," mused an officer alongside me. "What do you think—a lieutenant at forty-five years of age—what do you think?" sighed this harrowed soul. "A hero at forty-five years—I did not enter the service to be a hero at forty-five years. I told the Secretary a while ago that when I died all I wanted on my tombstone was 'Lieutenant B——, U.S. Navy, Buncoed.'"

Do not imagine that this deep sentiment interferes with my old friend—he likes to think aloud about his trouble—and it's a good fashion very much affected by all the sea-going men.

A fat little 'prentice boy became confidential with me after introducing me to many ship's mysteries, and said, "We are starving aboard this ship—we have nothing to eat."

With surprise I turned on him—such a startling statement—to think of Uncle Sam's starving these brave "bullies" of his, but I kept back my laugh, for the fat little rascal was positively greasy, and his trousers strained about his legs.

I can see the Captain up on the bridge, forty feet above the water; the executive, Mr. Rodgers, a sharp-visaged gentleman, who goes speeding about the ship hunting up trouble for any man who looks comfortable; and the engineer officers, who come up out of the coal and grease for a breath of fresh air. The marine sergeant in charge of the after deck sweats badly as he strides about, buttoned up to the last gasp. The young officers in the steerage show me a strange Burmah goddess—in marble—kept under lock and key, except when they make their big medicine, and they told me the story, but my lips are ice.

Sometimes things do happen, but they are little things. The black cat fell overboard one morning, or the fox terrier who inhabits up forward chased him overboard—we do not know which. An alarm was promptly given—it would never do to have a black cat lose her life in such a way, for black cats in particular are portentous things even when alive, but dead ones are something awful. Who knows what might happen after that?

So a boat was lowered and the big battleship *Iowa* temporarily abandoned the block-ade of Havana and steamed in a circle, hunting one lost black cat. The cat came alongside, pawing the water frantically, and was rescued by a jackie, who went down the sea ladder and grabbed her just in time.

With night it comes cool, and the officers and men sit smoking in the shadow of the superstructure, gazing at the lights of Havana—we might be a yachting party off Newport, only we are not. The guns are all shotted and the watch on deck lies about them on the deck, all ready on the instant. There are two little tubs of Spanish gunboats in the harbor, which come outside and are chased back. They appear to be monkeying with us, but if they get near enough we will saw them off and have fun with them.

The sea is like the water in your bath tub; the iron plate of the *Iowa* is like a griddle—the sky is more red than blue, and a mosquitoe's wings would create a hurricane in the air.[1]

The United States Battleship Iowa *Making Seventeen Knots an Hour*

NIGHT SPECIAL.

AN AMERICAN PAPER FOR THE AMERICAN PEOPLE

NEW YORK EVENING JOURNAL

NIGHT SPECIAL

NO. 5,620—P. M.

NEW YORK, WEDNESDAY, APRIL 6, 1898.

PRICE ONE CENT.

RIOTING IN HAVANA.

VOLUNTEERS HAVE POSSESSION OF STREETS—2,000 AMERICANS IN PERIL.

This Is Why McKinley's Message Was Held. To Rescue All the Citizens Now in the Cuban Capital.

LEE CABLED THAT PUBLICATION OF MESSAGE WOULD MEAN A MASSACRE.

WASHINGTON, April 6.--The cause of the postponement of the President's message is now definitely known. General Lee sent four cablegrams to the President, notifying him that a riot had broken out in Havana, and that the volunteers have possession of the streets.

If the message should go in now, Lee says a massacre might take place. In view of this the President will not assume the responsibility of sending in the message.

Two thousand Americans, Lee says, are now in Havana and more are expected.

The agents of the Plant line of steamers have also called on the President to-day and told him that owing to the disability of one of their steamers yesterday, the Olivette, they could not undertake to transport all Americans from Havana to-day. General Lee told the President that the situation was grave in the extreme and that he could not make his appeal for a postponement of the message too strong.

He sent his cablegrams in duplicate to provide against possible accident.

As soon as President McKinley received the information he sent for leading members of the Senate and House and told them that he felt compelled from a sense of duty and in order not to needlessly imperil the lives of thousands of Americans to heed General Lee's appeal.

It is now understood that the message will not go in until Monday.

NO MESSAGE TILL MONDAY.

WASHINGTON, APRIL 6.—THE PRESIDENT'S MESSAGE WILL NOT BE SENT TO CONGRESS UNTIL MONDAY.

THE POSTPONEMENT OF THE SENDING OF THE PRESIDENT'S MESSAGE TO CONGRESS CAME WITH SUCH SUDDENNESS THAT THE SENATE HAD NO TIME TO CONSIDER. IT HAD TO BE ACTED ON UNDER THE SPUR OF THE MOMENT.

THE LIVES OF AMERICAN CITIZENS WERE SUPPOSED TO BE IN DANGER.

UNDER OTHER CIRCUMSTANCES THE SENATE WOULD HAVE RISEN IN REVOLT. IT WOULD HAVE DEFIED THE PRESIDENT, BUT IT DID NOT CARE TO STAND SPONSOR FOR A POSSIBLE MASSACRE.

AT FIRST THERE WAS A DISPOSITION TO DOUBT THE ACCURACY OF THE STATEMENT THAT LEE HAD ASKED FOR DELAY, BUT SENATOR DAVIS ASSURED THE SENATORS THAT THERE WAS NO DOUBT ABOUT THE GENUINENESS OF THE APPEAL FOR DELAY.

IT IS RUMORED HERE THAT GENERAL LEE HAS LEFT HAVANA. NO ONE WHO KNOWS LEE BELIEVES IT.

FLYING SQUADRON UNDER SAILING ORDERS?

Washington, April 6.—It was reported at the Navy Department at noon that orders had been issued to the flying squadron to proceed to sea.

The report was soon afterward denied and immediately there came another report, apparently authoritative, that the squadron had as a matter of fact been told to go to sea at once under sealed orders.

Contradictory rumors, which the Bureau of Navigation failed to set at rest, alternated in quick succession.

CRUISER CINCINNATI AGROUND AT KEY WEST.

Key West, Fla., April 6.—The cruiser Cincinnati went aground this morning in eighteen feet of water about 300 feet from Taylor's wharf. The Merritt & Chapman wrecking craft Right Arm an hour or two later towed her out to deep water.

The Cincinnati was detailed for patrol duty last night and met with the mishap coming in early this morning.

She was moving slowly and is not damaged.

BERNABE TO STAY FOR THE PRESENT.

Washington, April 6.—The Spanish Minister, Senor Polo y Bernabe, will not ask for his passports until after war is declared. The withdrawal of Ministers is the last break made between countries.

It is denied that vandals have thrown mud on the sign of the Spanish Legation, as reported. The Spanish have been treated with the utmost courtesy on every hand.

SYMPATHY OF BRITAIN WITH U. S.

London, April 6. The British Government has formally assured the United States that Great Britain fully and cordially sympathizes with Brita's position with reference to Cuba.

QUEEN IN CONTROL; SPAIN MAY BACK DOWN.

Washington, April 6.—It is learned that one cause of the President's determination not to send his message until Monday is that the Queen Regent of Spain has taken the situation into her own hands and there is reason to believe that she may accede to all of the demands of the United States.

An opportunity is to be given her to do this.

QUEEN HERSELF SAW WOODFORD.

London, April 6.—A dispatch from Madrid sent across the border for transmission by telegraph says that the Queen Regent in person, through the German Ambassador, made a proposition of peace to Minister Woodford.

IS ONE OF OUR CONSULS A SPANISH PRISONER?

Washington, April 6.—There is a rumor here that one of the American Consuls in Cuba has been held a Spanish prisoner. No official confirmation of the report can be had.

EXTRA

NO 14 LATEST NEWS

HURRYING AWAY AMERICAN REFUGEES

TWO CRUISERS LEAVE HAVANA WITH MANY ESCAPING AMERICANS ON BOARD.

WASHINGTON, April 6.—The Bache and Mangrove have sailed from Havana for Key West with a large number of American refugees, according to information received at the Navy Department this afternoon.

The Mangrove and Bache will return to the Cuban capital to-morrow.

QUEEN MAY PROCLAIM ARMISTICE.

LONDON, April 6.—A dispatch from Madrid this afternoon says that the Queen Regent will issue a proclamation to-morrow announcing an armistice in Cuba. This action may cause resignation in the Cabinet.

FRUIT STEAMER RESCUES AMERICANS.

KINGSTON, Jamaica, April 6.—The Boston Fruit Company's steamer Barnstaple, chartered by the United States Consul here, sailed this morning and has taken off the American citizens at Santiago de Cuba.

REPORT THAT WE HAVE PURCHASED TWO LINERS.

The Lokal Anzeiger, of Berlin, says that a representative of the United States has purchased the Hamburg-American Line steamships Columbia and Normannia. Emil A. Boas, the agent of the line in this city, has learned that he had no confirmation of the report.

INSURGENTS MOVING TOWARD HAVANA.

Havana, April 6.—General Garcia has gone to join General Gomez, and their forces, numbering 4,000 men, are now believed to be moving for the provinces of Matanzas and Havana.

This movement has much significance. It means that the insurgents are prepared to act as soon as the Spanish-American clash comes.

THREE MORE SHIPS IN COMMISSION.

Mayflower, Wasp and Tecumseh Added to the Mosquito Fleet To-day.

The Mayflower, the Wasp and the Tecumseh, of the mosquito fleet, were put in commission at the Navy Yard this afternoon.

Lieutenant Ward took charge of the Wasp, Lieutenant Southland is in charge of the Tecumseh and the Mayflower was placed in charge of Commander McKenzie.

Sailing orders are expected hourly for these auxiliary craft from the Navy Department. They will join the Key West fleet.

The Barton, recently returned from Boston, is now in dry dock No. 1, and will be put in proper shape for service at the earliest possible moment.

WAR RUSH ON MORGAN LINERS.

El Sol and El Norte Unloading with All Possible Dispatch, to Be Equipped as Cruisers.

The two Morgan line steamers, El Sol and El Norte, purchased by the Government, are being rapidly unloaded at pier No. 25, North River. They will then be sent to the Brooklyn Navy Yard.

The Navy Department will accept the crews of the two boats if they are willing to remain. Both captains say they will accept any berths above that of common seaman.

The other two ships of the line, the El Rio and El Sud, purchased by the Government, have been ordered back here from southern waters to discharge their cargoes.

Wigwags from the Blockade

Modern war is supposed to be rapid, and we Americans think time is money, but this war seems to be the murder of time, the slow torture of opportunity.

For seven long days and nights I have been steaming up and down on the battle-ship *Iowa*, ten miles off the harbor of Havana. The *Mayflower* got on the land side of a British tramp and warned her off, and a poor Spanish fishing-schooner from Progreso, loaded with rotting fish, was boarded from a boat's crew from us. When the Captain saw the be-cutlassed and bepistolled "tars" he became badly rattled, and told the truth about himself. A Spaniard has to be surprised into doing this. He had been many days out, his ice was gone, and his fish were "high." He wanted to make Havana, telling the boarding officer that the people of Havana were very hungry. He had been boarded five times off the coast by our people; so the Lieutenant—who had just gotten out of bed, by the way—told him to take his cargo of odors out into the open sea, and not to come back again.

The appalling sameness of that pacing up and down before Havana worked on the nerves of everyone from Captain to cook's police. We are neglected; no one comes to see us. All the Key West trolley-boats run to the Admiral's flag (the *New York*) and we know nothing of the outside. We speculate on the *Flying Squadron*, the *Oregon*, the army, and the Spanish. I had an impression that I was not caught young enough to develop a love of the sea, which the slow passage of each day reinforces. I had formed a habit of damning the army for its procrastination, but in my heart of hearts I yearned for it. I wanted to hear a "shave-tail" bawl; I wanted to get some dust in my throat; I want to kick the dewy grass, to see a sentry pace in the moonlight, and to talk the language of my tribe. I resist it; I suppress myself; but my homely old first love came to haunt me, waking and sleeping—yes, even when I looked at that mountain of war material, that epitome of modern science, with its gay white officers, who talk of London, Paris, China and Africa in one breath. Oh, I know I should fall on the neck of the first old "dough-boy" or "yellow-leg" I see, and I don't care if he was making bread at the time.

The Morro light has been extinguished, but two powerful searches flash back and forth against the sky.

"Good things to sail by," the navigator says. "We can put them out when the time comes."

Another purpose they serve is that "Jackie" has something to swear at as he lies by his loaded gun—something definite, something material to swear at. Also, two small gun-

43

Wigwagging with a Dark Lantern—After-Deck

Watching the Big Search-Lights in Havana

AN AMERICAN PAPER FOR THE AMERICAN PEOPLE

NEW YORK JOURNAL

NIGHT. | NO. 5,664—P. M. | NEW YORK, FRIDAY, MAY 20, 1898. | PRICE ONE CENT. | **BASEBALL.**

CERVERA MUST FIGHT!

COMBINED ATTACK BY SAMPSON AND SCHLEY.

One Will Take the Windward, the Other the Yucatan Passage to Santiago---No Escape for the Spanish Fleet.

WASHINGTON, May 20.---At 4:30 o'clock the Navy Department posted the following official bulletin:

"The Department has information which is believed to be authentic that the Spanish squadron under Admiral Cervera is at Santiago de Cuba."

It is believed that orders have already been transmitted to Admiral Sampson at Key West directing an attack upon the Spanish fleet from both east and west.

In this case the two reorganized fleets under Sampson and Schley will swoop down upon Santiago by way of the Windward and Yucatan passages.

It will be impossible for the Spaniards to avoid a battle. If they remain in Santiago the American fleets will bottle them up, and if an attempt is made to escape from the harbor they will fall a prey to either Sampson or Schley.

ECRET ARMS CHAMBER FOUND ON SPANISH SHIP.

A secret chamber containing arms and ammunition was found to-day in the Argonauta, the steamship captured three

---

EXTRA

NO. 11

| NEW YORK | - | - | 2 |
| ST. LOUIS | - | - | 6 |

SCORE BY INNINGS

NEW YORK	1	0	0	0	0	0	0	0—2
ST. LOUIS	0	3	0	2	1	0	0	0—6

BROOKLYN-LOUISVILLE GAME POSTPONED.

The Brooklyn-Louisville game, at Louisville, has been postponed on account of wet grounds. Two games will be played to-morrow.

AT BALTIMORE—Pittsburg 3, Baltimore 1.
AT CHICAGO—Chicago 1, Washington 6.
AT CINCINNATI—Boston 5, Cincinnati 4.
AT CLEVELAND—End 8th inning—Philadelphia 4, Cleveland 3.
(FOR DESCRIPTION OF BASEBALL AND RACING SEE PAGE 9.)

SHOT HIMSELF IN WAGNER CAR OFFICE.

Harry Dankhard, nineteen years old, of No. 17 East Twenty-fourth street, a clerk in the employ of the Wagner Palace Car Company at Forty-fourth street and Vanderbilt avenue, accidentally shot himself in the left leg in the company's office late this afternoon. He was taken to the Flower Hospital.

TROOP SHIP YUCATAN SAILS.

The Ward Line steamer Yucatan, chartered as a troop ship by the Government, sailed to-day for Tampa. She will embark troops for Cuba.

PROSTRATED IN ENTERING CHICKAMAUGA.

New Yorkers Fall Victims of the Intense Heat While Marching Into Camp. Nearly 40,000 Men Now Assembled.

Chickamauga National Park, Georgia, May 20.—The nearly 40,000 volunteers encamped here, many of them from Northern States, wearing heavy woolen clothing, suffered greatly to-day from the intense heat, and the ambulance corps were kept busy carrying off the victims of prostration.

Eighteen members of the Fifth New York Volunteers were prostrated this afternoon while marching into the camp through Rossville Gap.

Chattanooga, Tenn., May 20.—Thirty-three thousand soldiers are now at Chickamauga, and 10,000 are expected in to-day.

The arrivals to-day have been the Second Missouri, 1,037 men; the First New Hampshire, 1,000 men, and Battery B, Pennsylvania Light Artillery. The Fourteenth New York arrived late in the night and was taken to Chickamauga late this afternoon.

F. K. McBeady, a private in the Twelfth New York, died this morning of delirium tremens. He was buried within three hours after death in the National Cemetery here by a detachment from his regiment.

Lieutenant-Colonel John Jacob Astor and General Breckenridge are expected here to-night.

Some of the soldiers are giving the police great trouble. The officers say very lenient with the men, a large number of whom proceed to become intoxicated soon after arrival. Owing to the hot climate they cannot gauge their drinking. The city police are powerless to preserve order.

It is claimed that two members of the Twelfth New York last night held up a prominent physician and rifled his pockets. They were arrested, but released by request of the Colonel commanding, who promised not to grant them any leave hereafter.

Commanders have been assigned to all the army corps.
New England still fears a Spanish warship surprise.
There are now nearly 40,000 troops in camp at Chickamauga.
The Senate has passed the Auxiliary Naval Bill.
The volunteer army now numbers 100,000.
Battery K has left Fort Wadsworth for Tampa.
The patrol boat Sarasota has been sunk in collision at Key West.
The Eighth Regiment is ready to leave for the South.

boats develop a habit of running out of the harbor—not very far, and with the utmost caution, like a boy who tantalizes a chained bear. And at places in the town smoke arises.

"What is it?" asks the Captain of marines.

"Big tobacco factories working overtime for us," replies Dr. Crandell.

I was taken down into the machinery of the ship. I thought to find in it some human interest. Through mile after mile of underground passages I crawled and scrambled and climbed amid wheels going this way and rods plunging that, with little electric lights to make holes in the darkness. Men stood about in the overpowering blasts of heat, sweating and greasy and streaked with black—grave, serious persons of superhuman intelligence—men who have succumbed to modern science, which is modern life. Daisies and trees and the play of sunlight mean nothing to these—they knew when all three were useful, which was enough. They pulled the levers, opened the shut-cocks, showered coal into the roaring white hells under the boilers; hither and yon they wandered, bestowing motherlike attention on rod and pipe. I talked to them, but they developed nothing except pre-occupied professionalism. I believe they fairly worshipped that throbbing mass of mysterious iron; I believe they loved this bewildering power which they control. Its problems entranced them; but it simply stunned me. At last when I stood on deck I had no other impression but that of my own feebleness, and, as I have said, felt rather stunned and stimulated. Imagine a square acre of delicate machinery plunging and whirling and spitting, with men crawling about in its demon folds. It is not for me to tell you more.

Don't waste your sympathy on these men below decks—they will not thank you; they will not even understand you. They are modern—are better off than "Jackie" and his poor wandering soul—they love their iron baby, so leave them alone with their joy. Modern science does not concern itself about death.

The *Iowa* will never be lost to the nation for want of care. By night there are dozens of trained eyes straining into the darkness, the searches are ready to flash, and the watch on deck lies close about its shotted guns. Not a light shows from the loom of the great battleship. Captain Evans sits most of the time on a perch upon the bridge, forty feet above the water-line. I have seen him come down to his breakfast at eight bells with his suspenders hanging down behind, indicating that he had been jumped out during the night.

The executive officer, Mr. Rogers, like the machinery down below, never sleeps. Wander where I would about the ship, I could not sit but a few moments before Mr. Rogers would flit by, rapid and ghost-like—a word here, an order there, and eyes for every-thing and everybody. Behind, in hot pursuit, came stringing along dozens of men hunting for Mr. Rogers; and this never seemed to let up—mid-night and mid-day all the same. The thought of what it must be is simply horrible. He has my sympathy—nervous prostration will be his reward—yet I greatly fear the poor man is so perverted, so dehumanized, as positively to like his life and work.

Naval officers are very span in their graceful uniforms, so one is struck when "at quarters" the officers commanding the turrets appear in their dungaree, spotted and soiled. The *Iowa* has six turrets, each in charge of an officer responsible for its guns and hoisting-gear, delicate and complicated. In each turret is painted "Remember the Maine." The gun-captains and turret-men acquire a strange interest and pride in their charges, hanging about them constantly.

Two gun-captains in the forward turret used to sit on the great brown barrels of the 12-inch rifles just outside the posts, guarding them with jealous care; for it is a "Jackie" trick to look sharply after his little spot on shipboard and to promptly fly into any stranger who defiles it in any way. At times these two men popped back into their holes like prairie-dogs. It was their hope and their home, that dismal old box of tricks, and it may be their grave. I was going to die with them there, though I resolutely refused to live with them. However, the *Iowa* is unsinkable and unlickable, and the hardware on the forward turret is fifteen inches thick, which is why I put my brand on it. So good luck to Lieutenant Van Duzer and his merry men.

"Jackie," the prevailing thing on a man-of-war, I fail to comprehend fully. He is a strong-visaged, unlicked cub, who grumbles and bawls and fights. He is simple, handy, humorous, and kind to strangers, as I can testify. The nearest he ever comes to a martial appearance is when he lines up at quarters to answer "here!" to his name, and there is just where he doesn't martialize at all. He comes barefooted, hat on fifty ways, trousers rolled up or down, and everything blowing wide. He scratches his head or stands on one foot in a ragged line, which grins at the spectators in cheerful heedlessness and he looks very much gratified when it is all over. His hope is for a bang-up sea-fight, or two roaring days of shore liberty, when he can "tear up the peach" with all the force of his reckless masculinity.

The marine, or sea-soldier, has succumbed to modern conditions, and now fights a gun the same as a sailor-man. He manages to retain his straight-backed discipline, but is overworked in his two-fold capacity. This "soldier and sailor too" is a most interesting man to talk to, and I wish I could tell some of his stories. He marches into the interior of China or Korea to pull a minister out of the fire—thirty or forty of him against a million savages, but he gets his man. He lies in a jungle hut on the isthmus or a "dobie" house on the west coast while the microbes and the "dogoes" rage.

But it's horribly alike to me, so I managed to desert. The *Cushing*, torpedoer, ran under our lee one fine morning, and I sneaked on board, bound for the flag-ship—the half-way station between us and Cayo Hueso. We plunged and bucked about in the roaring waves of the gulf, and I nearly had the breakfast shaken out of me. I assure you that I was mighty glad to find the lee of the big cruiser *New York*.

On board I found that the flag-ship had had some good sport on the previous day shelling some working parties in Matanzas. Mr. Zogbaum, staff artist for Harper's, and Richard Harding Davis had seen it all, note-book in hand. I was stiff with jealousy; but it takes more than one fight to make a war—so here's hoping.

Under the circumstances that then existed, the blockade of Cuba was a belligerent act for an official declaration was not to be forthcoming for another three days, April 25, 1898.

Remington's "landing" on the *Iowa* and his seven days at sea were ended, much to his gratification, and he was "dumped" on dry land.

At that particular period no attempt was made by the powers in Washington or by the heads of the military to do anything but dampen the enthusiasm that existed in the ranks. Spain had too powerful a force stationed in Cuba to attempt an invasion, at least until the whereabouts of the Spanish navy could be determined and a showdown effected. As a matter of fact we did not have a trained force large enough to stage a full-scale invasion of the island. It was ill equipped. The arms and munition were in the main obsolete and the uniforms and clothing left much to be desired for an army that was slated to participate in tropical warfare.

Remington sent the following dispatch to the New York *Journal* which was published April 27, 1898:

This little sketch, taken from the woolen clothed, heavily packed men of the Twenty-fifth, illustrates what they will NOT carry if they go to Cuba. The soldiers themselves will rid themselves of it, though the authorities should do so before soldiers are sent south.

Time, would, of necessity, be the only course. Aside from the fleet that was stationed there, little was happening at Key West, for it was much too small an area to encamp a full-scale invasion force. Some of the military whiled away their time there, but it was in the main the navy personnel who awaited the day when a more definite action would be forthcoming.

Remington went about his work, sketching and forwarding the drawings to the New York *Journal*. Boredom settled over the men like a pall. In the way of satire Remington wrote a story, "The War Dreams," that appeared in *Harper's Weekly*, May 7, 1898.

The War Dreams

At the place far from Washington where the gray, stripped warships swing on the tide, and toward which the troop-trains hurry, there is no thought of peace. The shore is a dusty, smelly bit of sandy coral, and the houses in this town are built like snare-drums; they are dismal thoroughly, and the sun makes men sweat, and wish to God they were somewhere else.

But the men in the blue uniforms are young, and Madame Beaulieu, who keeps the restaurant, strives to please, so it came to pass that I attended one of these happy-go-lucky banquets. The others were artillery officers, men from off the ships, with a little sprinkle of cavalry and infantry just for salt. They were brothers, and yellow-jack—hellish heat—bullets, and the possibility of getting mixed up in a mass of exploding iron had been discounted long back in their schoolboy days perhaps. Yet they are not without sentiment, and are not even callous to all these, as will be seen, though men are different and do not think alike—less, even, when they dream.

"Do you know, I had a dream last night," said a naval officer.

"So did I."

"So did I," was chorused by the others.

"Well, well!" I said. "Tell your dreams. Mr. H—, begin."

"Oh, it was nothing much. I dreamed that I was rich and old, and had a soft stomach, and I very much did not want to die. It was a curious sort of feeling, this very old and rich business, since I am neither, nor even now do I want to die, which part was true in my dream."

"I thought I was standing on the bluffs overlooking the Nile. I saw people skating, when suddenly numbers of hippopotamuses—great masses of them—broke up through the ice and began swallowing the people. This was awfully real to me. I even saw Mac there go down one big throat as easily as a cocktail. Then they came at me in a solid wall. I was

SPORTING SPECIAL.

CIRCULATION OF THE JOURNAL WEDNESDAY, APRIL 20. **1,146,967** ETC. DEDUCTED.

AN AMERICAN PAPER FOR AMERICANS

BASEBALL EXTRA.

NEW YORK JOURNAL

NO. 5,636—P. M.   NEW YORK, FRIDAY, APRIL 22, 1898.   PRICE ONE CENT.

REAR-ADMIRAL SAMPSON REPORTS

HAVANA BLOCKADED!

OTHER CUBAN PORTS INVESTED.

ARMY BILL SIGNED BY THE PRESIDENT,

Report That Spanish Cruiser Alfonso XII. Has Been Sunk Not Confirmed.

Gunboat Nashville Fired First Gun of the War in Capturing a Spanish Ship.

EXTRA.

NO. 16

PHILADELPHIA -	13
NEW YORK - -	7

SCORE BY INNINGS.

PHILADELPHIA ...... 0 5 3 0 0 4 0 0 1—13
NEW YORK.......... 0 0 4 0 2 0 0 1 0—7

(FOR DESCRIPTION OF GAME SEE PAGE 5.)

END THIRD INNING—BROOKLYN 7, WASHINGTON 3

RESULTS AT BENNINGS.
FIRST RACE—First Fruit, Louise N., Festa.
SECOND RACE—Holden, Rhodymenia, Subject.
THIRD RACE—Sophomore, Nigger Baby, Ellerslie Belle.
FOURTH RACE—Charmius, Warrenton, Vigenta.
FIFTH RACE—Lucid, Alarum, Her Own.
SIXTH RACE—Vanity Fair, Athlete, St. George.

RESULTS AT NEWPORT.
FIRST RACE—King Barleycorn, Pat Garrett, Hadrian.
SECOND RACE—Baritaria, Commerce, Dora B.
THIRD RACE—Cecil, Ten Pins, Judge Baker.
FOURTH RACE—Imp. Richard J., Aunt Bird.

WINNERS AT MEMPHIS.
FIRST RACE—Dick Collins, Pirate Judge, John Mander.
SECOND RACE—Voyager, Yellow Jacket, Wheaton.
THIRD RACE—Goodrich, J. A. Gray, Fervor.

FAMOUS CRICKET PLAYER KILLED.
PHILADELPHIA, April 22.—William Jarvis, aged eighty-six, was run down and instantly killed by a Philadelphia and Reading train at Whitey station, near here, this morning. Mr. Jarvis was a famous cricket player and an authority on the game. He was credited with having introduced it here.

HOW THE KEY WEST FLEET GOT UNDER WAY.

Sixteen Ships Set Out for Cuba, Their Prows Pointed Toward Havana, in Early Morning—Detroit Follows at 1:30 P. M.

Key West, Fla., April 22.—Sixteen ships of the United States Navy, comprising the greater part of the North Atlantic Squadron, under Admiral Samp-

---

NASHVILLE BRINGS HER PRIZE INTO KEY WEST.

Buena Ventura Captured After a Chase in Which Two Shots Were Fired—Prize Is a Big Merchant Ship.

Key West, Fla., April 22.—The first gun was fired by an American war ship. The first prize taken is a Spanish merchantman.

The prize, the Buena Ventura, arrived here at 10:30 o'clock this morning, accompanied by her captor, the gunboat Nashville. They were greeted by cheering throngs.

The Buena Ventura was sighted by the American squadron while it was on its way to Key West this morning. The Nashville, a fleet gunboat, detached herself from the squadron and gave chase.

A shot was fired to give the merchantman warning that she was wanted. To this she paid no attention. Then came a second shot, and the Spanish officers, realising that matters were becoming serious, hastily hauled down their flag.

The Buena Ventura was sighted about 6 o'clock this morning seventeen miles southwest of Key West, and by 7 o'clock she was seen to be a two-masted, black-hulled ship flying the Spanish flag.

The Nashville at once gave chase and started full speed for the Spaniard. A moment later a gun was fired from the port battery of the Nashville, the shot striking the water a few hundred yards away.

The Spaniard at this time was half a mile from the Nashville, and she held her way, making no sign of having given the shot any attention.

For two minutes the Nashville continued the chase, and then tried another shot that passed apparently within a rod of the Spaniard's bow.

STOPPED AT THE SECOND SHOT.

The officer on the Spaniard's bridge at once reversed her engines while a man aft and hastily lowered her flag. At this the Nashville brought to alongside the Spaniard, having every gun, big and little, in the starboard broadside pointed at her.

Then a whaleboat was lowered, and Ensign Magruder, with a boarding crew of six men, was sent and took charge of the prize.

The torpedo boat Foote had run down in the wake of the Nashville, and brought to beside the Buena Ventura.

Continued on Second Page.

MADRID PAPER BIDS US BEWARE.

Imparcial Declares That the Guns of Spanish Batteries Are About to Speak.

Madrid, April 22.—The Imparcial, in a war editorial to-day, says:

"As we are writing, the war ships of the United States will have commenced to execute the ignoble crime decreed by Washington, namely, the blockade of Havana. But the guns of our batteries are about to speak. The moment has arrived to prove the endurance and courage of the army, which is so desirous of gaining glory.

"The first shot fired by the Yankees ought to be the signal for a complete unison of all Spaniards in defence of the fatherland. Spain has snatched victory from more perilous situations."

PARIS NOT IN PERIL OF SPAIN'S SHIPS.

At Any Rate, the Navy Department Professes to Have No Fear.

Ovation at Southampton.

Washington, April 22.—To all inquiries concerning the American Liner Paris, now crossing the Atlantic, Navy Department officials say there is no danger of her capture by Spain. No information will be given concerning the new cruiser Topeka, also said to be in danger of capture.

Southampton, April 22.—The American steamship Paris sailed for New York this afternoon on her last trip prior to her going into the service of the United States as a cruiser.

Scenes of the greatest enthusiasm attended her departure. She carried 136 passengers and a heavy cargo, including several quick-fire gun fittings.

As the Paris passed the dock heads all of the flags on the vessels lying at the wharves were dipped, and the men on board the Union line steamer Britain struck up "Yankee Doodle," which they sang at the tops of their voices.

The crew of the Paris cheered vociferously in acknowledgment.

M'KINLEY PROCLAIMS A BLOCKADE OF CUBA.

He Announces That All Ships Attempting to Enter Havana or Other Northern Ports Are Liable to Seizure.

Washington, April 22.—The following proclamation was issued by the President this afternoon:

"By the President of the United States, a proclamation:

"Whereas, By a joint resolution by Congress, and approved April 20, 1898, and communicated to the Government of Spain, it was demanded that the Government at once relinquish its authority and government in the island of Cuba and withdraw its land and naval forces from Cuba and Cuban waters, and the President of the United States was directed and empowered to use the entire land and naval forces of the United States, and to call into the actual service of the United States the militia of the several States, to such extent as might be necessary to carry said resolution into effect; and,

"Whereas, In carrying into effect said resolution the President of the United States deems it necessary to set on foot and maintain a blockade of the north coast of Cuba, including all ports on said coast between Cardenas and Bahia Honda, and the port of Cienfuegos, on the south coast of Cuba,

"Now, therefore, I, William McKinley, President of the United States, in order to enforce the said resolution, do hereby declare and proclaim that the United States of America has instituted, and will maintain a blockade of the north coast of Cuba, including ports on said coast, between Cardenas and Bahia Honra, and the port of Cienfuegos, on the south coast of Cuba, aforesaid in pursuance of the laws of the United States and the law of nations applicable to such cases.

"An efficient force will be posted, so as to prevent the entrance and exit of vessels from the ports aforesaid. Any neutral vessel approaching any of said ports or attempting to leave the same, without notice or knowledge of the establishment of such blockade, will be duly warned by the commander of the blockading force, who will indorse on his register the day and the date of such warning, where such indorsement was made; and if the same vessel shall again attempt to enter any blockaded port, she will be captured and sent to the nearest convenient port for such proceedings against her and her cargo as prize as may be deemed advisable.

"Neutral vessels lying in any of said ports at the time of the establishment

Continued on Second Page.

crazed with fear—I fled. I could not run; but coming suddenly on a pile of old railroad iron, I quickly made a bicycle out of two car-wheels, and flew. A young hippo more agile than the rest made himself a bike also; and we scorched on over the desert. My strength failed; I despaired and screamed—then I woke up. Begad, this waiting and waiting in this fleet is surely doing things to me!"

The audience laughed, guyed, and said let's have some more dreams, and other things. This dream followed the other things, and he who told it was an artillery man:

"My instincts got tangled up with one of those Key West shrimp salads, I reckon; but war has no terrors for a man who has been through my last midnight battle. I dreamed I was superintending two big 12-inch guns which were firing on an enemy's fleet. I did not know where this was. We got out of shot, but we seemed to have plenty of powder. The fleet kept coming on, and I had to do something, so I put an old super-annuated sergeant in the gun. He pleaded, but I said he was old, the case was urgent, it did not matter how one died for his country, etc.—so we put the dear old sergeant in the gun and fired him at the fleet. Then the battle became hot. I loaded soldiers in the guns and fired them out to sea, until I had no more soldiers. Then I began firing citizens. I ran out of citizens. But there were Congressmen around somewhere there in my dreams, and though they made speeches of protest to me under the five-minute rule, I promptly loaded them in, and touched them off in their turn. The fleet was pretty hard-looking by this time, but still in the ring. I could see the foreign sailors picking pieces of Congress-men from around the breech-blocks, and the officers were brushing their clothes with their handkerchiefs. I was about to give up, when I thought of the Key West shrimp salad. One walked conveniently up to me, and I loaded her in. With a last convulsive yank I pulled the lock-string, and the fleet was gone with my dream."

"How do cavalry men dream, Mr. B—?" was asked of a yellow-leg.

"Oh, our dreams are still strictly professional, too. I was out with my troop, being drilled by a big fat officer on an enormous horse. He was very red-faced, and crazy with rage at us. He yelled like one of those siren-whistles out there in the fleet.

"He said we were cowards, and would not fight. So he had a stout picket-fence made, about six feet high, and then, forming us in line, he said no cavalry was any good which could be stopped by any obstacle. Mind you, he yelled it at us like a siren. He said the Spaniards would not pay any attention to such cowards. Then he gave the order to charge, and we flew into the fence. We rode at the fence pell-mell—into it dashed our horses, while we sabred and shouted. Behind us now came the big colonel—very big he was now, with great red wings—saying above all the din, 'You shall never come back—

This little sketch taken from the ~~the~~ woolen clothed — heavily
packed men of the 25th — illustrates what they will N̲O̲T̲
carry if they go to Cuba. — The soldiers themselves will
rid themselves of it though — the authorities should
do so before ~~they~~ soldiers are sent South.

                        Frederic Remington

you shall never come back!' and I was squeezed tighter and tighter by him up to this fence until I awoke; and now I have changed my cocktail to a plain vermouth."

When appealed to, the infantry officer tapped the table with his knife thoughtfully: "My dream was not so tragic; it was a moral strain, but I suffered greatly while it lasted. Somehow I was in command of a company of raw recruits, and was in some trenches which we were constructing under fire. My recruits were not like soldiers—They were not young men. They were past middle age, mostly fat, and many had white side whiskers after the fashion of the funny papers when they draw banker types. I had a man shot, and the recruits all got around me; they were pleading and crying to be allowed to go home.

"Now I never had anything in the work but my pay, and am pretty well satisfied as men go in the work, but I suppose the American does not breathe who is averse to posses-

54

sing great wealth himself; so when one man said he would give me one million dollars in gold if I would let him go, I stopped to think. Here is where I suffered so keenly. I wanted the million, but I did not want to let him go.

"Then these men came up, one after the other, and offered me varying sums of money to be allowed to run away—and specious arguments in favor of the same. I was now in agony. Damn it! That company was worth nearly a hundred million dollars to me if I would let them take themselves off. I held out, but the strain was horrible. Then they began to offer me their daughters—they each had photographs of the most beautiful American girls—dozens and dozens of American girls, each one of which was a peach. Say, fellows, I could stand the millions. I never did 'gig' on the money, but I took the photographs, said, 'Give me your girls, and pull your freight!' and my company disappeared instantly. Do you blame a man stationed in Key West for it—do you, fellows?"

"Not by a damn sight!" sang the company, on its feet.

"Well, you old marine, what did you dream?"

"My digestion is so good that my dreams have no red fire in them. I seldom do dream; but last night, it seems to me, I recall having a wee bit of a dream. I don't know that I can describe it, but I was looking very intently at a wet spot on the breast of a blue uniform coat. I thought they were tears—women's tears. I don't know whether it was a dream or whether I really did see it."

"Oh, damn your dreams!" said the Doctor. "What is Congress doing from last reports?"

The Fighting Negro Regulars in Their Key West Camp

4. Tampa—The Wait for Action

The Tampa, Florida, area was chosen to be the focal point for future operations. Remington hied himself there for that was where the news would be and that was where "his soldiers" were to be encamped.

Tampa was, at that time, nothing more than "a city chiefly composed of derelict houses drifting on an ocean of sand."[1] Out of all proportion to the importance of the town or any influx of visitors who might normally have been expected to visit that area was the Tampa Bay Hotel. It was the brainchild of a real estate speculator, Morton F. Plant, who had had visions of great things which had never come to pass. The hotel rose in solitary and magnificent splendor from the desert that surrounded it. It was a "giant affair of ornamental brick and silver minarets," gingerbread, potted palms, and statuary. It was so enormous that an appetite could be worked up simply by "walking from the rotunda to the dining-room."[2] It was Victorian in the best tradition. The high and mighty took it over and it became the hub of all military, journalistic, and social life for there was no place else in Tampa to arouse one's interest. All high-ranking military men and their staffs were housed there, the best of the world's correspondents kept their headquarters informed of any worthwhile news or lack of it. Time slumbered on while the powers were deciding the next move. Mr. Richard Harding Davis described it as "The Rocking Chair" period of the war. With an array of magnificent talent whiling away endless days, Mr. Davis wrote that "the two men of greatest interest to the army of the rocking chairs were probably America's representative, Frederic Remington, and Great Britain's representative with our army, Captain Arthur H. Lee. These two held impromptu receptions at every hour of the day, and every man in the army either knew them or wanted to know them."[3]

For active journalists, Key West was a place of absolute boredom. A plunge in the bay, greasy breakfasts, a drive in a cab to see nothing.

A man comes along and says, "Remington's looking for you." There is only a triangle of streets where one can find him and I call at "Josh" Curry's first and then at Pendleton's

Left: *Captain Arthur H. Lee, R.A., Representing the British Army with the United States Forces at Tampa*

Center: *Richard Harding Davis, Correspondent of the London* Times, *at Tampa*

Right: *C. E. Akers, Correspondent of the London* Times, *at Tampa*

Left: *Lieut.-Col. Wallace F. Randolph, U.S.A., Commanding Field*
Artillery Brigade (Ten Batteries), Port Tampa, Florida
58
Right: *Lieutenant Count A. v. Goetzen, German Military Attaché*

Top Left: *Brigadier-General Guy V. Henry, U.S. Vols., Commanding 1st Brigade, 5th Corps, Tampa*

Top Right: *Major-General Joseph Wheeler, U.S. Vols., Commanding Cavalry Division, Tampa*

Bottom Left: *Major-General William R. Shafter, U.S. Vols., Commanding 5th Army Corps, Tampa*

Bottom Right: *Major-General James F. Wade, U.S. Vols., Now commanding 3rd Army Corps, Chickamauga*

News Store and read all the back numbers of the *Police Gazette* for the hundredth time and then call here at the Custom House and then look in at the Cable office. In the meantime Remington is looking for me a hundred yards in the rear. He generally gets to Josh's as I leave the Custom House.[4]

While others rocked, Remington busied himself with those things nearest to him, the soldier and the horse. He was at the dock painting the loading of the *Gussie,* an ancient side-wheeler, whose job it was to carry arms and supplies to the rebels in Cuba. The war's first attempt at such an operation was doomed to failure. Its leave-taking from Port Tampa was heralded with much fanfare. No security was enforced and it was said that upon her arrival off the coast of Cuba "it began to look as though every one in Cuba had come down to receive them ashore."

He sketched and painted the everyday routine of the army as it awaited the day their boring existence might end and they would be off to Cuba and have a go at the Spanish.

Time, red tape, rumors—these were dimming an enthusiasm which a short time before had been overflowing. Enthusiasm—Remington wrote of a typical event: "Soldiers Who Cry," *Harper's Weekly,* May 21, 1898.

Soldiers Who Cry

Yesterday I called at the Ninth Infantry Camp, and Colonel Powell told the following in the course of conversation, and it struck me as a new note. This regiment came from Plattsburg Barracks, New York, and when the order came to go the colonel asked his captains to draw up small details out of the companies which should be left behind to guard and look after the property of the government at Plattsburg.

The colonel drew these details up in line to instruct them in their duties, which he did at some length. He said he noticed tears running down the faces of some of the men, but it did not strike him seriously at the time. He dismissed the squad and left the building; but in a string behind him came the men, crying like children. One old mustached and grizzled chap was bawling as though at his mother's funeral; he begged, he pleaded, he implored the colonel by all his gods not to leave him behind. Others did the same, standing there crying, blubbering, and beseeching Colonel Powell not to make them stay behind. The old colonel was quite taken aback. He did not know just what to do. He liked the spirit, but the discipline had never had just this sort of a shock before, and it upset him. He told the men they had been detailed by their captains to stay behind to guard property because they were steady men. It did nothing but cause more pleading, more blubbering, and the colonel walked away. He did not tell me if he had a tear in his own eye when he turned his back, but the men had to be rounded sharply up and regularly made to stay. This is the kind of boys to follow the band, I say.

Remington's contribution to the record of army life during those drab days is invaluable.

United States Troops Practising Marching in the Palmetto

Top: *Field sketch for illustration which appears on Page 71*
Bottom: *Ninth Cavalry Colored Troops on Washing Duty in the Gulf*

With the Regulars at Port Tampa—Ninth United States Cavalry Skirmishing Through the Pines

With the Regulars at Port Tampa, Florida—Troopers of the Ninth United States Cavalry Taking Their Horses for a Dash into the Gulf

U. S. Signal Corps at Work

With the Regulars at Port Tampa, Florida—United States Cavalry Passing an Army Pack-Train on the Road

69

Left: *American Soldier—Fit for Fighting*
Right: *The Man Who Gives the Commands*

Squadron A in the War—Orders from Headquarters

The Soldier of Today Looks Businesslike

In the Hands of the Camp Barber at Tampa

5. With the Fifth Corps[1]*

I approach this subject of the Santiago campaign with awe, since the ablest correspondents in the country were all there, and they wore out lead-pencils most industriously. I know I cannot add to the facts, but I remember my own emotions, which were numerous, interesting, and, on the whole, not pleasant. I am as yet unable to decide whether sleeping in a mud-puddle, the confinement of a troop-ship, or being shot at is the worst. They are irritating, and when done on an empty stomach, with the object of improving one's mind, they are extravagantly expensive. However, they satisfied a life of longing to see men do the greatest thing which men are called on to do.

The creation of things by men in time of peace is of every consequence, but it does not bring forth the tumultuous energy which accompanies the destruction of things by men in war. He who has not seen war only half comprehends the possibilities of his race. Having thought of this thing before, I got a correspondent's pass, and ensconced myself with General Shafter's army to Tampa.

When Hobson put the cork in Cervera's bottle, it became necessary to send the troops at once, and then came the first shock of the war to me. It was in the form of an order to dismount two squadrons of each regiment of cavalry and send them on foot. This misuse of cavalry was compelled by the national necessities, for there was not at that time sufficient volunteer infantry equipped and in readiness for the field. It is without doubt that our ten regiments of cavalry are the most perfect things of all Uncle Sam's public institutions. More good honest work has gone into them, more enthusiasm, more intelligence, and they have shown more results, not excepting the new navy or the postal system.

The fires of hatred burned within me. I was nearly overcome by a desire to go off the reservation. I wanted to damn some official, or all officialism, or so much thereof as might be necessary. I knew that the cavalry officers were to a man disgusted, and thought

*Remington's own account.

74

they had been misused and abused. They recognized it as a blow at their arm, a jealous, wicked, and ignorant stab. Besides, the interest of my own art required a cavalry charge.

General Miles appeared at Tampa about that time, and I edged around toward him, and threw out my point. It is necessary to attack General Miles with great care and understanding, if one expects any success. "General, I wonder who is responsible for this order dismounting the cavalry?" I ventured.

I think the old man could almost see me coming, for he looked up from the reading of a note, and in a quiet manner, which is habitual with him, said, "Why, don't they want to go?" and he had me flat on the ground.

"Oh yes, of course! They are crazy to go! They would go if they had to walk on their hands!" I said, and departed. A soldier who did not want to go to Cuba would be like a fire which would not burn—useless entirely. So no one got cursed for that business; but it is a pity that our nation finds it necessary to send cavalry to war on foot. It would be no worse if some day it should conclude to mount "bluejackets" for cavalry purposes, though doubtless the "bluejackets" would sit tight. But where is the use of specialization? One might as well ask the nurse-girl to curry the family horse.

So the transports gathered to Port Tampa, and the troops got on board, and the correspondents sallied down to their quarters, and then came a wait. A Spanish war-ship had loomed across the night of some watch-on-deck off the Cuban coast. Telegrams flew from Washington to "stop where you are." The mules and correspondents were unloaded, and the whole enterprise waited.

Here I might mention a series of events which were amusing. The exigencies of the service left many young officers behind, and these all wanted, very naturally to go to Cuba and get properly shot, as all good soldiers should. They used their influence with the general officers in command; they begged, they implored and they explained deviously and ingeniously why the expedition needed their particular services to insure success. The old generals, who appreciated the proper spirit which underlay this enthusiasm, smiled grimly as they turned the young scamps down. I used to laugh to myself when I overheard these interviews, for one could think of nothing so much as the schoolboy days, when he used to beg off going to school for all sorts of reasons but the real one, which was a ball-game or a little shooting trip.

Presently the officials got the Spanish war-ship off their nerves, and the transports sailed. Now it is so arranged in the world that I hate a ship in a compound, triple-expansion, forced-draught way. Barring the disgrace, give me ten days on the island. Do any-

The Gussie Expedition—First Embarkation of United States Troops for Cuba, at Port Tampa, May 11

thing to me, but do not have me entered on the list of a ship. It does not matter if I am to be the lordly proprietor of the finest yacht afloat, make me a feather in a sick chicken's tail on shore, and I will thank you. So it came about that I did an unusual amount of real suffering in consequence of living on the SEGURANCA during the long voyage to Cuba. I used to sit out on the after-deck and wonder why, at my time of life, I could not so arrange my affairs that I could keep off ships. I used to consider seriously if it would not be a good thing to jump overboard and let the leopard-sharks eat me, and have done with a miserable existence which I did not seem to be able to control.

When the first landing was made, General Shafter kept all the correspondents and the foreign military attaches in his closed fist, and we all hated him mightily. We shall probably forgive him, but it will take some time. He did allow us to go ashore and see the famous interview which he and Admiral Sampson held with García, and for the first time to behold the long lines of ragged Cuban patriots, and I was convinced that it was no mean or common impulse which kept up the determination of these ragged, hungry souls.

Then on the morning of the landing at Daiquiri the soldiers put on their blanket rolls, the navy boats and launches lay by the transports, and the light ships of Sampson's fleet ran slowly into the little bay and turned everything loose on the quiet, palm-thatched village. A few fires were burning in the town, but otherwise it was quiet. After severely pounding the coast, the launches towed in the long lines of boats deep laden with soldiery, and the correspondents and foreigners saw them go into the overhanging smoke. We held our breath. We expected a most desperate fight for the landing. After a time the smoke rolled away, and our people were on the beach, and not long after some men climbed the steep hill on which stood a block-house, and we saw presently the stars and stripes break from the flag-staff. They are Chinese! said a distinguished foreign soldier; and he went to the other side of the boat, and sat heavily down to his reading of our artillery drill regulations.

We watched the horses and mules being thrown overboard, we saw the last soldiers going ashore, and we bothered General Shafter's aide, the gallant Miley, until he put us all on shore in order to abate the awful nuisance of our presence.

No one had any transportation in the campaign, not even colonels of regiments, except their good strong backs. It was for every man to personally carry all his own hotel accommodations; so we correspondents laid out our possessions on the deck, and for the third time sorted out what little we could take. I weighed a silver pocket-flask for some

time, undecided as to the possibility of carriage. It is now in the woods of Cuba, or in the ragged pack of some Cuban soldier. We had finally three days of crackers, coffee, and pork in our haversacks, our canteens, rubber ponchos, cameras, and six-shooter—or practically what a soldier has.

I moved out with the Sixth Cavalry a mile or so, and as it was late afternoon, we were ordered to bivouac. I sat on a hill, and down in the road below saw the long lines of troops pressing up the valley toward Siboney. When our troops got on the sand beach, each soldier adjusted his roll, shouldered his rifle, and started for Santiago, apparently by individual intuition.

The troops started, and kept marching just as fast as they could. They ran the

Spaniards out of Siboney, and the cavalry brigade regularly marched down their retreating columns at Las Guasimas, fought them up a defile, outflanked, and sent them flying into Santiago. I think our army would never have stopped until it cracked into the doomed city in column formation, if Shafter had not discovered this unlooked-for enterprise, and sent his personal aide on a fast horse with positive orders to halt until the "cracker-line" could be fixed up behind them.

In the morning I sat on the hill, and still along the road swung the hard-marching columns. The scales dropped from my eyes. I could feel the impulse, and still the Sixth was held by orders. I put on my "little hotel equipment," bade my friends good-by, and "hit the road." The sides of it were blue with cast-off uniforms. Coats and overcoats were strewn about, while the gray blankets lay in the camps just where the soldiers had gotten up from them after the night's rest. This I knew would happen. Men will not carry what they can get along without, unless they are made to; and it is a bad thing to "make" American soldiers, because they know what is good for them better than any one who sits in a roller-chair. In the tropics, mid-day marching under heavy knits, kills more men than damp sleeping at night. I used to think the biggest thing in Shafter's army was my pack.

It was all so strange, this lonely tropic forest, and so hot. I fell in with a little bunch of headquarters cavalry orderlies, some with headquarters horses, and one with a mule dragging two wheels, which I cannot call a cart, on which General Young's stuff was tied. We met Cubans loitering along, their ponies loaded with abandoned soldier-clothes. Staff-officers on horseback came back and said that there had been a fight on beyond, and that Colonel Wood was killed and young Fish shot dead—that the Rough Riders were all done to pieces. There would be more fighting, and we pushed forward, sweating under the stifling heat of the jungle-choked road. We stopped and cracked cocoanuts to drink the milk. Once, in a sort of savanna, my companions halted and threw cartridges into their carbines. I saw two or three Spanish soldiers on ahead in some hills and brush. We pressed on; but as the Spanish soldiers did not seem to be concerned as to our presence, I allowed they were probably Cubans who had taken clothes from dead Spanish soldiers, and so it turned out. The Cubans seem to know each other by scent, but it bothered the Northern men to make a distinction between Spanish and Cuban, even when shown Spanish prisoners in order that they might recognize their enemy by sight. If a simple Cuban who stole Spanish soldier clothes could only know how nervous it

(text continues on page 84)

Frederic Remington in the Train of General Shafter

A Spanish Picket Post

81

The Right of the Road

made the trigger fingers of our regulars, he would have died of fright. He created the same feeling that a bear would, and the impulse to pull up and let go was so instinctive and sudden with our men that I marvel more mistakes were not made.

At night I lay up beside the road outside of Siboney, and cooked my supper by a soldier fire, and lay down under a mango-tree on my rubber, with my haversack for a pillow. I could hear the shuffling of the marching troops, and see by the light of the fire near the road the white blanket rolls glint past its flame-tired, sweaty men, mysterious and silent too, but for the clank of tin cups and the monotonous shuffle of feet.

In the early morning the field near me was covered with the cook-fires of infantry, which had come in during the night. Presently a battery came dragging up and was greeted with wild cheers from the infantry, who crowded up to the road. It was a great tribute to the guns; for here in the face of war the various arms realized their inter-dependence. It is a solace for cavalry to know that there is some good steady infantry in their rear, and it is a vast comfort for infantry to feel that their front and flanks are covered, and both of them like to have the shrapnel travelling their way when they go in.

At Siboney I saw the first wounded Rough Riders, and heard how they had behaved. From this time people began to know who this army doctor was, this Colonel Wood. Soldiers and residents in the Southwest had known him ten years back. They knew Leonard Wood was a soldier, skin, bones, and brain, who travelled under the disguise of a doctor, and now they know more than this.

Then I met a fellow-correspondent, Mr. John Fox, and we communed deeply. We had not seen this fight of the cavalry brigade, and this was because we were not at the front. We would not let it happen again. We slung our packs and most industriously plodded up the Via del Rey until we got to within hailing distance of the picket posts, and he said: "Now, Frederic, we will stay here. They will pull off no more fights of which we are not a party of the first part." And stay we did. If General Lawton moved ahead, we went up and cultivated Lawton; but if General Chaffee got ahead, we were his friends, and gathered at his mess fire. To be popular with us it was necessary for a general to have command of the advance.

But what satisfying soldiers Lawton and Chaffee are! Both seasoned, professional military types. Lawton, big and long, forceful, and with iron determination. Chaffee, who never dismounts but for a little sleep during the darkest hours of the night, and whose head might have been presented to him by one of William's Norman barons. Such a head! We used to sit around and study that head. It does not belong to the period; it

Bringing up the Guns Under Fire

Major-General Henry W. Lawton, U.S. Vols. Leader of the Expeditions
South and North of Manila—Against Santa Cruz and San Isidro

87

*Brigadier-General Adna R. Chaffee, U.S. Vols., Command-
ing 2nd Division, 5th Corps*

is remote, when the race was young and strong; and it has "warrior" sculptured in every line. It may seem trivial to you, but I must have people "look their part." That so many do not in this age is probably because men are so complicated; but "war is a primitive art," and that is the one objection I had to von Moltke, with his simple student face. He might have been anything. Chaffee is a soldier.

The troops came pouring up the road, reeking under their packs, dusty, and with their eyes on the ground. Their faces were deeply lined, their beards stubby, but their minds were set on "the front"—"on Santiago." There was a suggestion of remorseless striving in their dogged stepping along, and it came to me that to turn them around would require some enterprise. I thought at the time that the Spanish commander would do well to assume the offensive, and marching down our flank, pierce the centre of the straggling column; but I have since changed my mind, because of the superior fighting ability which our men showed. It must be carefully remembered that, with the exception of three regiments of Shafter's army, and even these were "picked volunteers," the whole command was our regular army-trained men, physically superior to any in the world, as any one will know who understands the requirements of our enlistment as against that of conscript troops; and they were expecting attack, and praying devoutly for it. Besides, at Las Guasimas we got the moral on the Spanish.

Then came the "cracker problem." The gallant Cabanais pushed his mules day and night. I thought they would go to pieces under the strain, and I think every packer who worked on the Santiago line will never forget it. Too much credit cannot be given them. The command was sent into the field without its proper ratio of pack-mules, and I hope the blame of that will come home to some one some day. That was the direct and only cause of all the privation and delay which became so notable in Shafter's operations. I cannot imagine a man who would recommend wagons for a tropical country during the rainy season. Such a one should not be censured or reprimanded; he should be spanked with a slipper.

So while the engineers built bridges, and the troops made roads behind them, and until we got "three days' crackers ahead," for the whole command, things stopped. The men were on half-rations, were out of tobacco, and it rained, rained, rained. We were very miserable.

Mr. John Fox and I had no cover to keep the rain out, and our determination to stay up in front hindered us from making friends with any one who had. Even the private soldiers had their dog-tents, but we had nothing except our two rubber ponchos. At

Top: *Captain Allyn Capron, U.S.A.*
Bottom: *American Soldiers Messing*

evening, after we had "bummed" some crackers and coffee from some good-natured officer, we repaired to our neck of woods, and stood gazing at our mushy beds. It was good, soft, soggy mud, and on it, or rather in it, we laid one poncho, and over that we spread the other.

"Say, Frederic, that means my death; I am subject to malaria."

"Exactly so, John. This cold of mine will end in congestion of the lungs, or possibly bronchial consumption. Can you suggest any remedy?"

"The fare to New York," said John, as we turned into our wallow.

At last I had the good fortune to buy a horse from an invalided officer. It seemed great fortune, but it had its drawback. I was ostracized by my fellow-correspondents.

All this time the reconnaissance of the works of Santiago and the outlying post of Caney was in progress. It was rumored that the forward movement would come, and being awakened by the bustle, I got up in the dark, and went gliding around until I managed to steal a good feed of oats for my horse. This is an important truth as showing the demoralization of war. In the pale light I saw a staff-officer who was going to Caney, and I followed him. We overtook others, and finally came to a hill overlooking the ground which had been fought over so hard during the day. Capron's battery was laying its guns, and back of the battery were staff-officers and correspondents eagerly scanning the country with fieldglasses. In rear of these stood the hardy First Infantry, picturesquely eager and dirty, while behind the hill were the battery horses, out of harm's way.

The battery opened and knocked holes in the stone fort, but the fire did not appear to depress the rifle-pits. Infantry in the jungle below us fired, and were briskly answered from the trenches.

I had lost my canteen and wanted a drink of water, so I slowly rode back to a creek. I was thinking, when along came another correspondent. We discussed things, and thought Caney would easily fall before Lawton's advance, but we had noticed a big movement of our troops toward Santiago, and we decided that we would return to the main road and see which promised best. Sure enough, the road was jammed with troops, and up the hill of El Poso went the horses of Grimes's battery and under whip and spur. Around El Poso ranch stood Cubans, and along the road the Rough Riders—Roosevelt's now, for Wood was a brigadier.

The battery took position, and behind it gathered the foreigners, naval and military, with staff-officers and correspondents. It was a picture such as may be seen at a manoeuvre. Grimes fired a few shells toward Santiago, and directly came a shrill screaming shrapnel from the Spanish lines. It burst over the Rough Riders, and the manoeuvre picture on the

The Charge at El Caney

Grimes's Battery Going Up El Pozo Hill

92

The Scream of the Shrapnel

93

Shrapnel Coming Up the Road

hill underwent a lively change. It was thoroughly evident that the Spaniards had the range of everything in the country. They had studied it out. For myself, I fled, dragging my horse up the hill, out of range of Grimes's inviting guns. Some as gallant soldiers and some as daring correspondents as it is my pleasure to know did their legs proud there. The tall form of Major John Jacob Astor moved in my front in jack-rabbit bounds. Prussian, English, and Japanese correspondents, artists, all the news, and much high-class art and literature, were flushed, and went straddling up the hill before the first barrel of the Dons. Directly came the warning scream of No. 2, and we dropped and hugged the ground like star-fish. Bang! right over us it exploded. I was dividing a small hollow with a distinguished colonel of the staff.

"Is this thing allowed, Colonel?"

"Oh, yes, indeed!" he said. "I don't think we could stop those shrapnel."

And the next shell went into the battery, killing and doing damage. Following shell were going into the helpless troops down in the road, and Grimes with-drew his battery for this cause. He had been premature. All this time no one's glass could locate the fire of the Spanish guns, and we could see Capron's smoke miles away on our right. Smoky powder belongs with arbalists and stone axes and United States ordnance officers, which things all belong in museums with other dusty rust.

Then I got far up on the hill, walking over the prostrate bodies of my old friends the Tenth Cavalry, who were hugging the hot ground to get away from the hotter shrapnel. There I met a clubmate from New York, and sundry good foreigners, notably the Prussian (Von Goetzen), and that lovely "old British salt" Paget, and the Japanese major whose name I could never remember. We sat there. I listened to much expert artillery talk, though the talk was not quite so impressive as the practice of that art.

But the heat—let no man ever attempt that after Kipling's "and the heat would make your blooming eyebrows crawl."

This hill was the point of vantage; it overlooked the flat jungle, San Juan hills, Santiago, and Caney, the whole vast country to the mountains which walled in the whole scene. I heard the experts talk, and I love military science, but I slowly thought to myself this is not my art—neither the science of troop movement nor the whole land-scape. My art requires me to go down in the road where the human beings are who do these things which science dictates, in the landscape which to me is overshadowed by their presence. I rode slowly, on account of the awful sun. Troops were standing every-where, lying all about, moving regularly up the jungle road toward Santiago, and I wound my way along with them, saying, "Gangway, please."

"Before the Warning Scream of the Shrapnel"

96

The Temporary Hospital, Bloody Ford

97

War is productive of so many results, things happen so awfully fast, men do such strange things, pictures make themselves at every turn, the emotions are so tremendously strained, that what knowledge I had fled away from my brain, and I was in a trance; and do you know, cheerful reader, I am not going to describe a battle to you.

War, storms at sea, mountains, deserts, pests, and public calamities leave me without words. I simply said "Gangway" as I wormed my way up the fateful road to Santiago. Fellows I knew out West and up North and down South pass their word to me, and I felt that I was not alone. A shrapnel came shrieking down the road, and I got a drink of water from Colonel Garlington, and a cracker. The soldiers were lying alongside and the staff-officers were dismounted, also stopping quietly in the shade of the nearest bush. The column of troops was working its way into the battle-line.

"I must be going," I said, and I mounted my good old mare—the colonel's horse. It was a tender, hand-raised trotting-horse, which came from Colorado, and was perfectly mannered. We were in love.

The long columns of men on the road had never seen this condition before. It was their first baby. Oh, a few of the old soldiers had, but it was so long ago that this must have come to them almost as a new sensation. Battles are like other things in nature— no two the same.

I could hear noises such as you can make if you strike quickly with a small walking-stick at a very few green leaves. Some of them were very near and others more faint. They were the Mausers, and out in front through the jungle I could hear what sounded like a Fourth of July morning, when the boys are setting off their crackers. It struck me as new, strange, almost uncanny, because I wanted the roar of battle, which same I never did find. These long-range, smokeless bolts are so far-reaching, and there is so little fuss, that a soldier is for hours under fire getting into the battle proper, and he has time to think. That is hard when you consider the seriousness of what he is thinking about. The modern soldier must have moral quality; the guerilla is out of date. This new man may go through a war, be in a dozen battles, and survive a dozen wounds without seeing an enemy. This would be unusual, but easily might happen. All our soldiers of San Juan were for the most part of a day under fire, subject to wounds and death, before they even had a chance to know where the enemy was whom they were opposing. To all appearances they were apathetic, standing or marching through the heat of the jungle. They flattened themselves before the warning scream of the shrapnel, but that is the proper thing to do. Some good-natured fellow led the regimental mascot, which was a fice, or a fox-terrier. Really, the dog of war is a fox-terrier. Stanley took one through Africa. He is in all English regiments, and he is gradually getting into ours. His flag is short, but it sticks up straight on all occasions, and he is a vagabond. Local ties must set lightly on soldiers and fox-terriers.

Then came the light as I passed out of the jungle and forded San Juan River. The clicking in the leaves continued, and the fire-crackers rattled out in front. "Get down, old man; you'll catch one!" said an old alkali friend, and I got down, sitting there with the officers of the cavalry brigade. But promptly some surgeons came along, saying that it was the only safe place, and they began to dig the sand to level it. We, in consequence, moved out into the crackle, and I tied my horse with some others.

"Too bad, old fellow," I thought; "I should have left you behind. Modern rifle fire is rough on horses. They can't lie down. But, you dear thing, you will have to take your chances." And then I looked at the preparation for the field hospital. It was altogether too suggestive. A man came, stooping over, with his arms drawn up, and hands flapping downward at the wrists. That is the way with all people when they are shot through the body, because they want to hold the torso steady, because if they don't it hurts. Then the oncoming troops poured through the hole in the jungle which led to the San Juan River, which was our line of battle, as I supposed. I knew nothing of the plan of battle, and I have an odd conceit that no one else did, but most all the line-officers were schooled men, and they were able to put two and two together mighty fast, and in most instances faster than headquarters. When educated soldiers are thrown into a battle without understanding, they understand themselves.

As the troops came pouring across the ford they stooped as low as they anatomically could, and their faces were wild with excitement. The older officers stood up as straight as on parade. They may have known that it is better to be "drilled clean" than to have a long ranging wound. It was probably both ideas which stiffened them up so.

Then came the curious old tube drawn by a big mule, and Borrowe with his squad of the Rough Riders. It was the dynamite-gun. The mule was unhooked and turned loose. The gun was trundled up the road and laid for a shot, but the cartridge stuck, and for a moment the cheerful grin left the red face of Borrowe. Only for a moment; for back he came, and he and his men scraped and whittled away at the thing until they got it fixed. The poor old mule lay down with a grunt and slowly died.

(text continues on page 108)

At the Bloody Ford of the San Juan

American Soldiers Swimming to an Assault on Insurgent Intrenchments

How the Horses Died for Their Country at Santiago

A Bayonet Rush of the United States Troops

The Storming of San Juan—The Head of the Charge—Santiago de Cuba, July 1, 1898

107

Having reached the firing-line, many officers left their horses tied to the brush on the sands of San Juan River. Baggage and gun mules were turned loose, and stood stupidly about. There was a constant tweet of bullets coming through the trees from the Spanish position. One horse caught three almost in a bunch; another passed through him, and he lay down on his side, panting desperately. A big gun-mule lay on his side gasping, and another horse sat down like a dog, giving every evidence of great pain. A ball cut the skin on a mule's knee, but he only stamped the leg as though to get rid of a troublesome fly.

The thing about it which was strange to me was that the horses which were untouched seemed sleepy—they gave no evidence of excitement except a slight pricking of the ears toward the hill. One almost wondered if they suspected that things were not right. Even the blood which was all about on the sands, from horses and men, did not have its general effect of scaring them.

Why do not horses die for their country? We do not have a previous intention of so doing—the act is not voluntary. Well, possibly. Neither does a conscript die voluntarily, or a man put war-stamps on checks voluntarily, but it's for the country just the same. A mule does more work for his country and more suffering than a man. It also takes more revenue stamps to keep him going. But why speak of these things? It is sufficient to know that all soldiers respect and honor all mules.[2]

The fire was now incessant. The bullets came like the rain. The horses lay down one after another as the Mausers found their billets. I tried to take mine to a place of safety, but a sharp-shooter potted at me, and I gave up. There was no place of safety. For a long time our people did not understand these sharp-shooters in their rear, and I heard many men murmur that their own comrades were shooting from behind. It was very demoralizing to us, and on the Spaniards' part a very desperate enterprise to lie deliberately back of our line; but of course, with bullets coming in to the front by the bucketful, no one could stop for the few tailing shots. The Spaniards were hidden in the mango-trees, and had smokeless powder.

Now men came walking or were carried into the temporary hospital in a string. One beautiful boy was brought in by two tough, stringy, hairy old soldiers, his head hanging down behind. His shirt was off, and a big red spot shone brilliantly against his marble-like skin. They laid him tenderly down, and the surgeon stooped over him. His breath

Lying in the Road Before the Attack, San Juan

came in gasps. The doctor laid his arms across his breast, and shaking his head, turned to a man who held a wounded foot up to him, dumbly imploring aid, as a dog might. It made my nerves jump, looking at that gruesome hospital, sand-covered, with bleeding men, and yet it seemed to have fascinated me; but I gathered myself and stole away. I went down the creek, keeping under the bank, and then out into the "scrub," hunting for our line; but I could not find our line. The bullets cut and clicked around, and a

"I could hardly see our troops crouching in the grass beside me . . ."

sharp-shooter nearly did for me. The thought came to me, what if I am hit out here in the bush while all alone? I shall never be found. I would go back to the road, where I should be discovered in such case; and I ran quickly across a space that my sharp-shooting Spanish friend did not see me. After that I stuck to the road. As I passed along it through an open space I saw a half-dozen soldiers sitting under a tree. "Look out—sharp-shooter!" they sang out. "Wheet!" came a Mauser, and it was right next to my ear, and two more. I dropped in the tall guinea-grass, and crawled to the soldiers, and they studied the mango-trees; but we could see nothing. I think that episode cost me my sketch-book. I believe I lost it during the crawl, and our friend the Spaniard shot so well I wouldn't trust him again.

From the vantage of a little bank under a big tree I had my first glimpse of San Juan hill, and the bullets whistled about. One would tumble on a tree or ricochet from the earth, and then they shrieked. Our men out in front were firing, but I could not see them. I had no idea that our people were to assault the hill—I thought at the time such an attempt would be unsuccessful. I could see with my powerful glasses the white lines of the Spanish intrenchments. I did not understand how our men could stay out there under that gruelling, and got back into the safety of a low bank.

A soldier said, while his stricken companions were grunting around him, "Boys, I have got to go one way or the other, pretty damn quick." Directly I heard our line yelling, and even then did not suppose it was an assault.

Then the Mausers came in a continuous whistle. I crawled along to a new place and finally got sight of the fort, and just then I could distinguish our blue soldiers on the hill-top, and I also noticed that the Mauser bullets rained no more. Then I started after. The country was alive with wounded men—some to die in the dreary jungle, some to get their happy home-draft, but all to be miserable. Only a handful of men got to the top, where they broke out a flag and cheered. "Cheer" is the word for that sound. You have got to hear it once where it means so much, and ever after you will grin when Americans make that noise.

I followed on up the hill. Our men sat about in little bunches in the pea-green guinea-grass, exhausted. A young officer of the Twenty-fourth, who was very much excited, threw his arms about me, and pointing to twenty-five big Negro infantrymen sitting near, said, "That's all—that is all that is left of the Twenty-fourth Infantry," and the tears ran off his mustache.

Farther on another officer sat with his arms around his knees. I knew him for one of these analytical chaps—a bit of a philosopher—too highly organized—so as to be morose. "I don't know whether I am brave or not. Now there is S—; he don't mind this sort of thing. I think—"

"Oh, blow your philosophy!" I interrupted. "If you were not brave, you would not be here."

The Spanish trenches were full of dead men in the most curious attitudes, while about on the ground lay others, mostly on their backs, and nearly all shot in the head. Their set teeth shone through their parted lips, and they were horrible. The life never runs so high in a man as it does when he is charging on the field of battle; death never seems so still and positive.

Troops were moving over to the right, where there was firing. A battery came up and went into position, but was driven back by rifle fire. Our batteries with their smoky powder could not keep guns manned in the face of the Mausers. Then, with gestures much the same as a woman makes when she is herding chickens, the officers pushed the men over the hill. They went crawling. The Spanish were trying to retake the hill. We were short of ammunition. I threw off my hat and crawled forward to have a look through my glass at the beyond. I could hardly see our troops crouching in the grass beside me, though many officers stood up. The air was absolutely crowded with Spanish bullets. There was a continuous whistle. The shrapnel came screaming over. A ball struck in front of me, and filled my hair and face with sand, some of which I did not get out for days. It jolted my glass and my nerves, and I beat a masterly retreat, crawling rapidly backwards, for a reason which I will let you guess. The small-arms rattled; now and then a wounded man came back and started for the rear, some of them shot in the face, bleeding hideously.

"How goes it?" I asked one.

"Ammunition! ammunition!" said the man, forgetful of his wound.

I helped a man to the field hospital, and got my horse. The lucky mare was untouched. She was one of three animals not hit out of a dozen tied or left at the hospital. One of these was an enormous mule, loaded down with what was probably officers' blanket rolls, which stood sidewise quietly as only a mule can all day, and the last I saw of him he was alive. Two fine officers' chargers lay at his feet, one dead and the other unable to rise, and suffering pathetically. The mule was in such an exposed position that I did not care to unpack him, and Captain Miley would not let any one shoot a horse, for fear of the demoralizing effect of fire in the rear.

112

"The Wounded, Going to the Rear, Cheered the Ammunition."

A trumpeter brought in a fine officer's horse, which staggered around in a circle. I saw an English sabre on the saddle, and recognized it as Lieutenant Short's, and indeed I knew the horse too. He was the fine thoroughbred which that officer rode in a Madison Square military tournament last winter, when drilling the Sixth Cavalry. The trumpeter got the saddle off, and the poor brute staggered around with a bewildered look in his eager eyes, shot in the stifle-joint, I thought; and then he sat down in the creek as a dog would on a hot day. The suffering of animals on a battlefield is most impressive to one who cares for them.

I again started out to the hill, along with a pack-train loaded with ammunition. A mule went down, and bullets and shells were coming over the hill aplenty. The wounded going to the rear cheered the ammunition, and when it was unpacked at the front, the soldiers seized it like gold. They lifted a box in the air and dropped it on one corner, which smashed it open.

"Now we can hold San Juan hill against them garlics—hey, son!" yelled a happy cavalryman to a doughboy.

"You bet—until we starve to death."

"Starve nothin'—we'll eat them gun-teams."

"Well, well," I said, "I have no receipt for licking the kind of troops these boys represent. And yet some of the generals wanted to retreat."

Having had nothing to eat this day, I thought to go back to headquarters camp and rustle something. Besides, I was sick. But beyond the hill, down the road, it was very dangerous, while on the hill we were safe. "Wait for a lull; one will come soon," advised on old soldier. It was a curious thing that battle firing comes like a big wind, and has its lulls. Now it was getting dark, and during a lull I went back. I gave a wounded man a ride to the field hospital, but I found I was too weak myself to walk far. I had been ill during the whole campaign, and latterly had fever, which, taken together with the heat, sleeping in the mud, marching, and insufficient food, had done for me.

The sight of that road as I wound my way down it was something I cannot describe. The rear of a battle. All the broken spirits, bloody bodies, hopeless, helpless suffering which drags its weary length to the rear, are so much more appalling than anything else in the world that words won't mean anything to one who has not seen it. Men half naked, men sitting down on the road-side utterly spent, men hopping on one foot with a rifle for a crutch, men out of their minds from sunstroke, men dead, and men dying. Officers came by white as this paper, carried on rude litters made by their devoted

In the Rear of the Battle—Wounded on the San Juan Road

soldiers, or borne on their backs. I got some food about ten o'clock and lay down. I was in the rear at headquarters, and there were no bullets and shells cracking about my ears, but I found my nerves very unsettled. During the day I had discovered no particular nervousness in myself, quite contrary to my expectations, since I am a nervous man, but there in the comparative quiet of the woods the reaction came. Other fellows felt the same, and we compared notes. Art and literature under Mauser fire is a jerky business; it cannot be properly systematized. I declared that I would in the future paint set pieces for dining-rooms. Dining-rooms are so much more amusing than camps. The novelist allowed that he would be forced to go home and complete "The Romance of a Quart Bottle." The explorer declared that his treatise on the "Flora of Bar Harbor" was promised to his publishers.

Soldiers always joke after a battle. They have to loosen the strings, or they will snap. There was a dropping fire in the front, and we understood our fellows were intrenching. Though I had gotten up that morning at half past three, it was nearly that time again before I went to sleep. The fever and the strong soldier-coffee banished sleep; then, again, I could not get the white bodies which lay in the moonlight, with the dark spots on them, out of my mind. Most of the dead on modern battle-fields are half naked, because of the first-aid bandage. They take their shirts off, or their pantaloons, put on the dressing, and die that way.

It is well to bear in mind the difference in the point of view of an artist or a correspondent, and a soldier. One has his duties, his responsibilities, or his gun, and he is on the fiiring line under great excitement, with his reputation at stake. The other stalks through the middle distance, seeing the fight and its immediate results, the wounded; lying down by a dead body, mayhap, when the bullets come quickly; he will share no glory; he has only the responsibility of seeing clearly what he must tell; and he must keep his nerve. I think the soldier sleeps better nights.

The next day I started again for the front, dismounted, but I only got to El Poso Hill. I lay down under a bank by the creek. I had the fever. I only got up to drink deeply of the dirty water. The heat was intense. The re-enforcing troops marched slowly up the road. The shells came railroading down through the jungle, but these troops went on, calm, steady, like true Americans. I made my way back to our camp, and lay there until nightfall, making up my mind and unmaking it as to my physical condition, until I concluded that I had "finished."

"The Biggest Thing in Shafter's Army Was My Pack."

117

6. Heroic Americans

The following story appeared in *Harper's Monthly*, April 1900. Except for the few novels that Remington wrote, most of his other writings were authentic to the core. Despite exhaustive research, I have not come upon a single clue regarding the authenticity of the characters in this story, but I am sure that Major Kessel and Oestreicher were real soldiers.

They Bore a Hand

When Mrs. Kessel with the two children saw the troops pack up and entrain their horses, she had plenty of things to do for the Major besides control her feelings. It had happened so many times before that it was not a particularly distinct sensation; but the going forth of an armed man is always thrilling—yes, even after twenty years of it. She did not think, I imagine, but she knew many wives of regular army officers whom Congress had forgotten, after the dead heroes had been heralded up and down the land and laid away. The "still small voice" of the army widow doesn't make the halls of Congress yell with rage at the stern facts. But she was accustomed, since the year of their marriage, to the departure of her besabred husband, and that was the "worse" for which she married him. The eldest girl was as near twenty as I can tell about such things. They were excited by the fast moving of events, and the flash of steel had benumbed their reflective quality, but papa was a soldier, and Spain had to be licked. Who could do it better than papa, Oestreicher, his orderly trumpeter, and the gallant Third, those nimble athletes who took the three bareback horses over the hurdles in the riding-hall? Who could withstand the tearing charge down the parade with the white blades flashing? Nothing but Oestreicher with his trumpet could stop that.

    Oestreicher had told them a thousand times that papa could lick any one under any conceivable circumstances. They very well knew that he had followed the flying Arapaho village far into the night, until he had captured everything; they were familiar with the niceties of the Apache round-up at San Carlos, because Oestreicher had handed the Major a six-shooter at the particular instant; and the terrible ten days' battle with the revengeful Cheyennes, when the snow was up to the horses' bellies, had been done to death by the orderly. Papa had been shot before, but it hadn't killed him, and they had never heard of "yellow-jack" on the high plains. Papa did all this with Oestreicher to help him, to be sure, for the orderly always declared himself a full partner in the Major's doings, and divided the glory as he thought best.

Oestreicher, orderly trumpeter, was white and bald. He never stated any recollections of the time before he was a soldier. He was a typical German of the soldier class; a fierce red in the face, illuminated by a long yellowish-white mustache, but in body becoming a trifle wobbly with age. He had been following the guidon for thirty-seven years. That is a long time for a man to have been anything, especially a trooper.

Oh yes, it cannot be denied that Oestreicher got drunk on pay-days and state occasions; but he was too old to change; in his day that thing was done. Also, he had love-affairs, of no very complex nature. They were never serious enough for the girls to hear of. Also, he had played the various financial allurements of the adjoining town, until his "final statement" would be the month's pay then due. But this bold humanity welled up in Oestreicher thoroughly mixed with those soft virtues which made every one in trouble come to him. He was a professional soldier, who knew no life outside a Sibley or a barrack, except the Major's home, which he helped the Major to run. On the drill-ground the Major undoubtedly had to be taken into account, but at the Major's quarters Oestreicher had so close an alliance with madam and the girls that the "old man" made a much smaller impression. A home always should be a pure democracy.

The Kessel outfit was like this: It was "military satrap" from the front door out, but inside it was "the most lovable person commands," and Oestreicher often got this assignment.

In the barracks Oestreicher was always "Soda"—this was an old story, which may have related to his hair, or his taste, or an episode—but no man in the troop knew why. When they joined, Oestreicher was "Soda," and traditions were iron in the Third.

Oestreicher and the Major got along without much friction. After pay-day the Major would say all manner of harsh things about the orderly because he was away on a drunk, but in due time Oestreicher would turn up smiling. Madam and the girls made his peace, and the Major subsided. He had got mad after this manner at this man until it was a mere habit, so the orderly trumpeter never came up with the court-martialling he so frequently courted, for which that worthy was duly grateful, and readily forgave the Major his violent language.

For days Oestreicher and the women folks had been arranging the Major's field-kit. The Major looked after the troops, and the trumpeter looked after the Major, just as he had for years and years before. When the train was about to pull out, the Major kissed away his wife's tears and embraced his children, while Oestreicher stood by the back door of the Pullman, straight and solemn.

"Now look out for the Major," solicited the wife, while the two pretty girls pulled the tall soldier down and printed two kisses on his red burnt cheeks, which he received in a disciplined way.

"Feed Shorty and Bill (dogs) at four o'clock in the afternoon, and see that they don't get fed out of mess hours," said the orderly to the girls, and the women got off the cars.

And Oestreicher never knew that Madam had told the Major to look out well for the orderly, because he was old, and might not stand things which he had in the earlier years. That did not matter, however, because it was all a day's work to the toughened old soldier. The dogs, the horses, the errands, the girls, the Major, were habits with him, and as for the present campaign—he had been on many before. It gave only a slight titillation.

Thus moved forth this atom of humanity with his thousands of armed countrymen to do what had been done before—set the stars and stripes over the frontier and hold them there. Indians, greasers, Spaniards—it was all the same, just so the K troop guidon was going that way.

The "shave-tails" could kick and cuss at the criminal slowness of the troop-train's progress, but Oestreicher made himself comfortable with his pipe and newspapers, wondering what kind of cousins Spaniards were to Mexicans, and speculating with another old yellowleg on the rough forage of Cuba.

So he progressed with the well-known events to Tampa and to Daiquiri, and here he fell over a very bad hurdle. He could brown hardtack in artful ways, he did not mind the mud, he could blow a trumpet to a finish, he could ride a horse as far as the road was cut out, but the stiffened knees of the old cavalryman were badly sprung under the haversack and blanket roll afoot.

"Get down."

The column was well out on the road to Siboney when the Major noted the orderly's distress: "Oestreicher, fall out—go back to the transport. You can't keep up. I will give you an order," which he did.

The poor old soldier fell to the rear of the marching men and sat down on the grass. He was greatly depressed, both in body and mind, but was far from giving up. As he sat brooding he noticed a ragged Cuban coming down the road on a flea-bitten pony, which was heavily loaded with the cast-off blankets of the volunteers. A quick lawless thought energized the broken man, and he shoved a shell into his Craig carbine. Rising slowly, he walked to meet the ragged figure. He quickly drew a bead on the sable patriot, saying, "Dismount—get down—you damn greaser!"

"*No entiendo.*"

"Get down!"

"*Por Dios, hombre, que va hacer?*" and at this juncture Oestreicher poked the Cuban in the belly with his carbine, and he slid off on the other side.

"Now run along—*vamose*—underlay—get a gait on you!" sang out the blue soldier, while the excited Cuban backed up the road, waving his hands and saying, "*Bandolero, ladrón, sin vergüenza! Porqué me roba el caballo?*"

To which Oestreicher simply said, "Oh, hell!"

Not for a second did Oestreicher know that he was a high agent of the law. Be it known that any man who appropriates property of your Uncle Samuel can be brought to book. It is hard to defend his action when one considers his motive and the horse.

The final result was that Oestreicher appeared behind the Third Cavalry, riding nicely, with his blanket roll before his saddle. The troops laughed, and the Major looked behind; but he quickly turned away, grinning, and said to Captain Hardier: "Look at the damn old orderly! If that isn't a regular old-soldier trick! I'm glad he has a mount; you couldn't lose him."

"Yes," replied the addressed. "You can order Oestreicher to do anything but get away from the Third. Can't have any more of this horse-stealing; it's demoralizing;" and the regiment plodded along, laughing at old "Soda," who sheepishly brought up the rear, wondering what justice had in store for him.

Nothing happened, however, and presently Oestreicher sought the Major, who was cursing his luck for having missed the fight at Las Guasimas. He condoled with the Major in the tactful way he had, which business softened things up. While the Major was watching him boil the coffee in the tin cups over a little "Indian fire," he put the order in the flames, and it went up in smoke.

"You old rascal!" was all the Major said, which meant that the incident was closed.

Right glad was the Major to have his orderly during the next week. The years had taught Oestreicher how to stick a dog-tent and make a bed, and how to cook and forage. Oestreicher's military conscience never vibrated over misappropriated things to eat, and Fagin could not have taught him any new arts.

Then came the fateful morning when the Third lay in the long grass under the hail of Mausers and the sickening sun. "Will the Major have some water?" said Oestreicher, as he handed over one canteen.

"You go lie down there with the men and don't follow me around—you will get shot," commanded Kessel; but when he looked around again, there was Oestreicher stalking behind. He could fool away no more energy on the man.

Then came the forward movement, the firing, and the falling men, and ahead strode the officer, waving his sword and shouting fiercely. Behind followed the jaded old trumpeter, making hard going of it, but determined to keep up. His eye was not on the blazing heights, but on the small of the Major's back, when the officer turned, facing him, and ran into his arms. Down over the Major's face came gushes of blood. He reeled—would have fallen but for the supporting arms of the soldier. The rush of men passed them.

They lay down in the grass. The orderly brushed the blood from the pale face, while he cut up a "first-aid" bandage and bound the wound. Then he gave him water; but the Major was far gone, and the orderly trumpeter was very miserable. Oestreicher replaced the Major's sword in its scabbard. Men came tottering back, holding on to their wounds.

"Say, Johnson," sang out Oestreicher to a passing soldier, "you ain't hit bad; gimme a lift with the Major here." The soldier stopped, while they picked up the unconscious officer and moved heavily off toward the Red Cross flag. Suddenly they lurched badly, and all three figures sank in the pea-green grass. A volley had found them. Johnson rolled slowly from side to side and spat blood. He was dying. Oestreicher hung on to one of his arms, and the bluish-mauve of the shirt sleeve grew slowly to a crimson lake. He sat helplessly turning his eyes from the gasping Johnson to the pale Major and the flaming hill-crest. He put his hat over the Major's face. He drank from his canteen. There was nothing to do. The tropical July sun beat on them until his head swam under the ordeal.

Presently a staff officer came by on a horse.

"There was nothing to do."

"Say, Captain," yelled the soldier, "come here. Major Kessel is hit in the head. Take him, won't you?"

"Oh, is that you?" said the one addressed as he rode up, for he remembered Kessel's orderly. Dismounting, the two put the limp form on the horse. While Oestreicher led the animal, the Captain held the nearly lifeless man in the saddle, bent forward and rolling from side to side. Thus they progressed to the blood-soaked sands beside the river, where the surgeons were working grimly and quickly.

It was a month before two pale old men got off the train at Burton, one an officer and the other a soldier, and many people in the station had a thrill of mingled pity and awe as they looked at them. Two very pretty girls kissed them both, and people wondered the more. But the papers next morning told something about it, and no policeman could be induced to arrest Oestreicher that day when he got drunk in Hogan's saloon, telling how he and the Major took San Juan hill.

Time wore on, wounds healed, and the troops came back from Montauk to the yelling multitudes of Burton, the home station. The winter chilled the fever out of their blood. The recruits came in and were pulled into shape, when the long-expected order for the Philippines came, and the old scenes were re-enacted just as they had happened in the Kessel household so many times before, only with a great difference: Oestreicher was detached and ordered to stay in the guard of the post. This time the Major, who was a Colonel now, settled it so it would stay settled. An order is the most terrible and potent thing a soldier knows. Oestreicher shed tears, he pleaded, he got the women to help him, but the Major stamped his foot and became ossified about the mouth.

Clearly there was only one thing left for Oestreicher to do in this case, and he did it with soldierly promptness. He got drunk—good and drunk—and the Third Cavalry was on its way to Manila. When the transport was well at sea from Seattle, the Colonel was reading a novel on the after-deck. A soldier approached him saluting, and saying, "I hope the Colonel won't get mad—"

The Colonel looked up; his eyes opened; he said, slowly, "Well—I—will—be—damned!" and he continued to stare helplessly into the cheerful countenance of Oestreicher, orderly trumpeter, deserter, stowaway, so food for courts martial. "How did you get here, anyway?"

Then the Colonel had a military fit. He cussed Oestreicher long and loud. Told him he was a deserter, said his long-service pension was in danger; and true it is that Oestreicher was long past his thirty years in the army, and could retire at any time. But

"I hope the Colonel won't get mad—"

through it all the Colonel was so astonished that he could not think—he could only rave at the tangle of his arrangements in the old orderly's interest.

"How did you get here, anyhow?"

"Came along with the train, sir—same train you were on, sir," vouchsafed the veteran.

"Well, well, well!" soliloquized the Colonel as he sat down and took up his novel. "Get out—I don't want to see you—go away," and Oestreicher turned on his heel.

Other officers gathered around and laughed at the Colonel.

"What am I to do with that old man? I can't court-martial him. He would get a million years in Leavenworth if I did. Damn these old soldiers, anyhow! They presume on their service. What can I do?"

"Don't know," said the junior Major. "Reckon you'll have to stay home yourself if you want to keep Oestreicher there."

It was plain to be seen that public sentiment was with the audacious and partly humorous orderly.

"Well—we will see—we will see!" testily jerked the old man, while the young ones winked at each other—long broad winks, which curled their mouths far up one side.

The Colonel has been seeing ever since. I have only just found out what he "saw," by a letter from an old friend of mine out in the Philippines, which I shall quote:

"You remember Colonel Kessel's old orderly—Oestreicher? Was with us that time we were shooting down in Texas. He was ordered to stay at Jackson Barracks, but he deserted. The men hid him under their bunks on the railroad train, and then let him on the transport at Seattle. Soldiers are like boys: they will help the wicked. One day he presented himself to the old man. Oh, say—you ought to have heard the old Nantan cuss him out—it was the effort of the old man's life! We sat around and enjoyed it, because Oestreicher is a habit with the Colonel. We knew he wouldn't do anything about it after he had blown off steam.

"Well, the night after our fight at Cabanatuan it was dark and raining. What do you suppose I saw? Saw the 'old man' in a nipa hut with a doctor, and between them old Oestreicher, shot through the head and dying. There was the Colonel sitting around doing what he could for his old dog-soldier. I tell you it was a mighty touching sight. Make a good story that—worked up with some blue lights and things. He sat with him until he died. Many officers came in and stood with their hats off, and the Colonel actually boohooed. As you know, boohooing ain't the 'old man's' long suit by a damn sight!"

There were occasions when Remington waxed enthusiastic over some particular military man. This man was not the general. He was usually the non-com or the shave-tail who had that certain quality to become a soldier of distinction and even, perhaps, to rise above that state of respect.

In *Harper's Weekly*, March 22, 1890, his article "Two Gallant Young Cavalrymen" appeared. Those concerned were Captain James Waterman Watson, cited for gallant service in action against the Indians near Salt River, Arizona, and Lieutenant Powhatan Henry Clark who was awarded the Medal of Honor for gallantry in action at Pima Mountains, May 3, 1886. Correspondence that I have seen indicates that these two and Remington were close personal friends and often went hunting together on the artist's frequent sojourns to the West.

Another example was his story "A Sergeant of the Orphan Troop" published in *Harper's Monthly*, August 1897. This concerned itself with Captain Dodd's troop of the Third Cavalry and their action against a brave band of Northern Cheyenne led by Dull Knife. The principal character was Carter Page Johnson, who also came into focus in "Vagabonding with the Tenth Horse," *The Cosmopolitan*, February 1897.

There were "Lieutenant Casey's Last Scout," "How the Worm Turned," and other writings by Remington of other memorable military men.

And so it came about that the artist's eye fell on Luther Rector Hare who had served his country well in action since the early 1870s. This is his story, short but true.

A Gallant American Officer

Colonel Hare is a long, lean, dried-out man, and he looks as though he came from Texas, which he did. He has had an interesting career since he left West Point in 1870. Nature intended him to pass his life on a horse, so she made him long in the gear and curved in the legs, as is best adapted to a saddle. His face has a high-nostriled, sharp-eyed, eager look—arranged to scent battle and to seek it.

He was Major Menill's adjutant in the Seventh Cavalry, and was one of the last men across the ford in Reno's repulse at the Little Big Horn. He it was who rode through the swarming Indians to rally Benteen and the pack-train—which he brought back to Reno's position.

He was with General Crook in his famous winter campaign against the Sioux in '76

The Death of Oestreicher

Colonel Hare

and was with General Forsyth at the battle of Wounded Knee. He chased the "Kid" over the sands of Arizona and led his troops in the Chicago riots down the acres of railroad track where it was supposed cavalry could not go.

At the outbreak of the Spanish war he was appointed colonel of the First Texas Cavalry, which he raised, drilled and organized, and sought vainly for service in Cuba. He had Rough Riders, and, if he had been allowed to go, would undoubtedly be Governor of Texas to-day. But, no! Hare is soldier all over—he couldn't be anything but a man on a horse. He wouldn't look right in a chair any more than General Miles does. They are not built that way, either of them.

After the surrender of Cuba, his regiment was disbanded and he went back to his troop, which was stationed at Vidado, outside of Havana; but this didn't suit, so he raised the Thirty-third U.S. Foot and went to the Philippines as colonel with the gallant Howz and Logan for field officers.

Immediately after his arrival in the Philippines, Colonel Hare was detailed to pursue one of the scattered forces of Aguinaldo's followers, who were retreating with Lieutenant Gilmore and various naval and military prisoners held by the Filipinos. After a most arduous and never-ceasing pursuit of many days, the Filipino force was overtaken and scattered, and Lieutenant Gilmore and his fellow-prisoners were rescued.

This was not only one of the most daring, continued and persistent pursuits of this war, but has few parallels in history. For weeks the men were without regular rations, without access to supplies of any kind; they had no changes of clothing; their shoes were worn out; men dropped from the ranks daily from sickness and exhaustion, and when the final battle took place, resulting in the rescue of Lieutenant Gilmore and his fellow-prisoners, Colonel Hare had only about one hundred and twenty-six men with him, and these men were in a most deplorable condition. Nothing but the most indomitable will power could have kept these men up to the pursuit until the end.

For this service General Otis has recommended him for a brigadier-general. The leading trait of Colonel Hare's nature is his modesty, as well befits his calling. In his report of the affair he claims as much credit as any private soldier in the command, and no more—which will show you how absurd he can be at times with his modesty.[1]

7. The Bronco Buster

During the year 1888 *Century Magazine* published a series of articles written by Theodore Roosevelt and illustrated by Frederic Remington. Later that year these were published in book form and entitled *Ranch Life and the Hunting-Trail*. It was Remington's first major work and most certainly had much effect in carrying him to the forefront with the top illustrators of the day. He was constantly in demand from that time on.

The paths of Remington and Roosevelt crossed many times during the next twenty years that remained for the artist, and resulted in a lasting friendship.

One of the close associations between the two men resulted from Remington's first bronze attempt—The Bronco Buster. The creation of this masterpiece is recalled by an intimate friend of the artist.

"Ruckstuhl, the sculptor, set up a tent on a vacant lot back of our place at New Rochelle, New York, and began in clay the construction of the half-size model for the heroic equestrian statue of General Hartrauft that now stands in bronze in front of the State-house at Harrisburg. It was Remington's first intimate view of sculpture in the making. The horse especially interested him. During the two months that the sculptor labored, Remington made daily visits to the Ruckstuhl tent. The following winter I was sitting one day in his studio watching him at an illustration for some story of Owen Wister's. He was working 'chic,' that is to say, without models, and was making his first marks in charcoal. His outline began to show a cow-boy in the foreground of a bar-room shooting toward the back of the picture, into the perspective of which ran the bar and its stampeding clientele. As it occurred to him that the bulking figure of the local egotist obscured too much of other interesting detail, he quickly dusted off the drawing and reversed his characters, thereby making the aggressor stand in the background and putting the victims to the front. With equal ease he could have put his cow-boy to either side of the room. I said to him:

" 'Frederic, you're not an illustrator so much as you're a sculptor. You don't mentally see your figures on one side of them. Your mind goes all around them.' "[1]

The Bronco Buster

Not long after that he bought a set of tools. Ruckstuhl sent him a supply of modeler's wax, and he began his "Bronco Buster." It was characteristic of the man that his first attempt should be a subject difficult enough as a technical problem to have daunted a sculptor of experience and a master of technique. His love of the work when he got at it, his marvelous aptitude for an art in which he had never had a single lesson, are some evidence that it was possibly his metier. His few bronze groups and figures that rapidly followed the "Bronco Buster," and his heroic equestrian monument of "The Pioneer" in Fairmont Park, are the work of one who surely would have excelled in sculpture if he had lived to follow it.

It is amazing to think that the result of the man's first attempt at sculpture should become symbolic of, one might say, the artist's entire career for it most certainly is one of his most popular works and is synonymous with the name Remington.

Approximately three years later, the Spanish-American War just ended, Theodore Roosevelt's Rough Riders were disbanding at Montauk, Long Island. Colonel Roosevelt recalled the incident:

"One afternoon, to my genuine surprise, I was asked out of my tent by Lieutenant-Colonel Brodie and found the whole regiment formed in hollow square, with the officers and color-sergeant in the middle. When I went in, one of the troopers came forward and on behalf of the regiment presented me with Remington's fine bronze 'The Bronco Buster.' There could have been no more appropriate gift from such a regiment, and I was not only pleased with it, but very deeply touched with the feeling which made them join in giving it."

Just a few days after Roosevelt's return home he sent the following telegram to Remington:

134

Form No. 1.

THE WESTERN UNION TELEGRAPH COMPANY.
INCORPORATED
21,000 OFFICES IN AMERICA.   CABLE SERVICE TO ALL THE WORLD.

This Company TRANSMITS and DELIVERS messages only on conditions limiting its liability, which have been assented to by the sender of the following message. Errors can be guarded against only by repeating a message back to the sending station for comparison, and the Company will not hold itself liable for errors or delays in transmission or delivery of Unrepeated Messages, beyond the amount of tolls paid thereon, nor in any case where the claim is not presented in writing within sixty days after the message is filed with the Company for transmission.
This is an UNREPEATED MESSAGE, and is delivered by request of the sender, under the conditions named above.

THOS. T. ECKERT, President and General Manager.

NUMBER   SENT BY   REC'D BY   (CHECK

4M   CN   67   paid

RECEIVED at New Rochelle, NY   9/19   1898

Dated Oyster Bay, L.I.

To Frederick Remington Esqr.

My dear Remington:

I think your letter pleased the Rough Riders who saw it, as much as their action pleased you. It was the most appropriate gift the Regiment could possibly have given me, and the one I would have valued most. I have long looked hungrily at that bronze, but to have it come to me in this precise way seemed almost too good.

Faithfully yours,

Theodore Roosevelt

Through the next eleven years that remained for Remington much correspondence passed between the two men and many were the invitations extended to the Remingtons to dine at the White House.

Almost ten years passed from date of the telegram when Remington received the following letter from the President of the United States. Typed on White House stationery it reads:

```
                                    Oyster Bay, N.Y.
                                    June 29, 1908

My dear Remington:
    I am mighty glad to get those three
photographs.  By George, that is a corking
bronze.  But do you know, I do not think
that any bronze you will ever make will
appeal to me more than the one of the bronco-
buster, which you know my regiment gave me.
I am mighty proud of it.  I prize also the
Man of the Stone Age which you sent me;
which, by the way, has a comic likeness to
a certain high personage whose name I won't
venture to put in writing, but will tell you
when I next see you.
                        Faithfully yours,
                        Theodore Roosevelt[2]
```

8. The Postwar Years

In the *Collier's Weekly* issue of February 25, 1899, the following short notice appeared:

Mr. Frederic Remington, artist and author, left New York February 11 for Havana, whither he goes as Special Correspondent of *Collier's Weekly*. He will forward a series of articles, written and illustrated by himself, on "The United States Army in Cuba." Remington's soldiers and Remington's horses are too well known to call for comment. He will portray with brush and pen the citizen soldiers who are now taking part in the military occupation of Cuba with graphic intensity and the same fidelity which characterizes his pictures of the Regular Army men and Western Life.

An entry in the diary of Miss Emma Caten adds for us a personal touch to the *Collier* quote: "On the 17th of February I was sent for to come to New Rochelle and stay while Fred went to Cuba for a month. Fred went much sooner than he expected but my visit was prolonged until the 8th of May."

Although Remington's assignment, as stated, was to cover the United States Army in Cuba, he found himself doing more on his impressions of a people emerging from a war fought for an independence they had never before tasted and with whose effects they were little equipped to cope.

The month since the end of the struggle had left little to be desired. Petty rivalries and a bungled policy had done little to endear the United States to a people who sorely needed our guidance and to whom we were offering little but confusion. The little patriot, General Calixto García, who had tried to do so much for his people, had been shunted aside and rapidly faded into obscurity. General Máximo Gómez was the man of the hour.

Such was the state of affairs in Cuba when Remington arrived there once again. In his own words and pictures he portrayed his observations of that depressing period in Cuba's history.

The Night Patrol

Under Which King?

Frederic Remington
Cuba

Havana Under Our Regulars

In *Collier's Weekly*, April 1, 1899, his story entitled "Havana Under Our Regulars" appeared.

I have just been there [Havana] again. This time I do not go feeling like a thief in the night or an unbidden guest, and I lived at the American Club, and sat at a mess of good old American soldiers, and ate roast beef rare. I saw the free Cubans greet their great hero with cheers as he marched in. I saw the new police being prepared to guard the interests of their own native community, and I called on General Ludlow at his office. There were no gold-laced or black-robed ones; no sentries, no fuss; nothing but a quiet engineer officer sitting at a desk before stacks of official papers, and very busy officers hurrying in and running out, all doing something useful. Soldiers patrolled the streets with loaded rifles, and nothing happened. Business men were figuring and discussing the future commercial development of the town. Everyone was hopeful, and the Cubans gradually adjusting themselves to their freedom. Too much cannot be expected at once of a people who have always lived under Spanish misrule and abuse. Cuba is not a new-born country, peopled by wood-cutting, bear-fighting, agricultural folks, who must be fresh and virtuous in order to exist. It is an old country, time worn, decayed, and debauched by thieving officials and fire and sword. . . .

The Cubans have never known civic rectitude; they have had no examples of honest, plain-dealing, public men; they are in the aggregate, the most ignorant people on earth, so far as letters go. But there are in the rural districts of Cuba an honest folk, whose only aim is to till the land in safety and to be allowed to reap what they shall sow. With good American governors to sit quietly by and see that no throats are cut, things will slowly come right.

Armed Neutrality in Cuba

Under Which King?

In the April 8, 1899, issue of *Collier's Weekly* an article entitled "Under Which King?" appeared. A portion of this article follows:

The rural districts of Cuba are full of soldiers of the Army of Liberation. They rack along the roads on their mice-like ponies—they stroll along with their blankets and rifles. They do not seem to have any definite purpose, and doubtless have none beyond locating fruitful fields.

Our regulars have organized a patrol of certain districts, and it only happened that I noticed a haughty reserve was maintained between these two soldiery as they passed. They lack a common language, and they hardly know what their official relations are to be.

Meanwhile the poor peasant of Cuba gives both the road. He is the most ignorant being I ever saw; he has been harried by soldiers until his soul shrinks at the sight of one. . . . The pathos of the spiritless people appeals to one's sympathies—makes him take them by the hand and reassure them. . . . He can understand that a warm heart only prompts the crackers but man on horseback he cannot approve.

In proportion to the people, the numbers who were in the Cuban army was small. The peasants, as it is the custom of the country to call them, were left helpless before the cruelty of the Spanish soldiers, and suffering also from the necessities of their own men in the field. Weyler concentrated them and intended to exterminate the race. Only the most vigorous, the most daring and enterprising, took to the *manigua*—only those with force and cunning enough to provide themselves with arms. The men of small holdings and large families stayed on the plot of ground, and they did the suffering for both parties. Among these are many Spaniards—men who came out to labor on the land; and never having experienced the quality of mercy, they did not expect it from the victors now. But, so far as I could learn, the Cuban soldiers had not disturbed these people—quite contrary to all preconceived notions; and it is greatly to their credit. To be sure, this fellow-feeling does not extend to those who served as guerillas for Spain. These the Cubans regard as murderers, and yearn to kill. . . .

The Triumph of a Conqueror[1]

"Gómez is coming to-day," said every one in Havana.

"Sure?"

"Yes—this time—sure."

He had been coming for a week—had been coming for three years, in fact; but he had often disappointed every one. Now I believed what was talked on the street. Taking a cab, I was rolled out to a suburb—name forgotten. We stopped where long lines of Cuban infantry stood on each side of the street. Behind these ranged the populace—men in black broadcloth, women white with face powder and brilliant with jewellery. . . . Everything was ready for the show.

Presently came a platoon of the Seventh United States Cavalry, and before I realized, in all the confusion, the Conqueror had come and had gone. He sat very stiff in his saddle, with his feet thrust out and his hand to his hat in acknowledgment of the cheers. His face was quite brown, his mustache white, and he was dressed in plain clothes of chocolate-colored cloth. The staff clattered behind, followed by a mounted band of "ours"; then interminable lines of Cuban infantry in columns of twos—mostly Negroes— but gotten up more smartly than General García's people down Santiago way.

It was all over for me in a few seconds, so far as the Conqueror was concerned. I noticed that his horse was small, because General Ludlow rode on his left, and he was on a big horse. Also Ludlow did not look like a conqueror. His bearing was modest to a noticeable extent.

The troops were passing for an hour, and I tried to break back into the city. Negro officers waved their machetes at my cabby and shouted fiercely. He was intimidated, and when I also d—— him properly in my native tongue for not getting me on my way, he was very miserable, but as I had no machete he wisely abided by the fear of those who had. Thus I was left thinking. I was no longer a Cuban sympathizer—that was clear. Things had come into my mind As They Are.

First: Gómez has a curious head—a very interesting head. It is fierce and warlike, and brown and mustached and goateed, and altogether Spanish-American, which does not mean "white man." His profile is a triangle with the jaw as the base. From his looks I should say his was not a great brain. Still that may not be so, in reality. As far as we know, he is a man of one idea—which happens in his case to be a very good one; and there is

Disbanding Gómez' Army—United States and Cuban Officers Inspecting Cuban Troops near Havana, Preparatory to Mustering Them Out of Service

The Return of Gómez to Havana

Frederic Remington

Havana

149

the force in the base of that triangle which has carried that one idea as far as the blood and iron and horse-flesh of Cuba could carry it.

Still, for all that, he would not have had the satisfaction of that morning's ride through the streets of Havana in a thousand years, except for what was represented by the platoon of cavalry in the front and the quiet man on his left. As I sat in my cab, gazing malevolently at my "cabby," I wondered if Gómez realized this in all its fulness. Time will tell this, and that only. So far he has been consistent. He wants us to "get out," "all the same" as the Spaniards, and I cannot see how we can help doing it. The old conqueror is not a patient man, but he had best study the story of Job very carefully, because those attributes are his only salvation. General Gómez has up until now done all that a man can do, and he makes his people do the same; and he must realize his hopes or we must lose our honor. If his aspirations fall withered to the ground, when the ballot should have susperseded the machete, it will be the regret of all the world.

Still, if all fails, the man who rode at his left hand when Gómez was a Conqueror comes of a race which has governed itself for over six hundred years—of a race which lived under a real democracy when it emerged from the northern forests of Europe, clad in skins, before Christianity or tempered steel was even known by them, and they will finally see that a Cuban man can till a field without fear of a dragonnade. They have never had any other idea concerning Cuba since they began to think about it long years ago. Spanish kings and Cuban bandits all look alike to the people of the United States, and they will handle one as they did the other if it becomes necessary. Patience is the watchword for Cuba.

"Rome was not built in a day."

Cuban Bandits in Santiago Province[2]

What was said would happen has happened. The turbulent part of García's old troops "has gone off the reservation." It is likely that more will go in other provinces, and then it is up to us. That is a part of the game. We opened a jackpot and we have got to stay.

We may feel comfortable from the fact that General Wood is commanding the province of Santiago. As a youngster he followed a more sprightly people over a worse and a bigger country, and he brought Geronimo's Apaches in. If he is furnished with what force he asks for he will in time quiet the country.

It is a mountainous region, covered with dense jungle, and utterly wild. The predatory bands of Negro soldiery have roamed it for years. They know its trails, its fastnesses, and its commissary resources. He will be in collusion with townspeople who will renew their ammunition, and they will have perfect information of our troop movements. They will ambuscade us in bands, and then disperse as individuals. The country is hot and not healthy. So much for their part, and, lest we forget, we will in all human probabilities do what we always have done under similar circumstances, send them a Peace Commission. They will grovel and whine and make "heap good talk," give them rations and ammunition, and ask them please to be good. Never having been good, they will go out in the jungle and laugh at us. They will feel that we are afraid of them. They will murder and rob some more, and then, having gotten through with this murderous foolish mess, which is traditional with us, General Wood will be asked to take up the "soldier's burden." He will not be given a proper force. There will ensue one of those desperate bush-whacking wars, with the bulk of the advantage on the guerillas' side. It is history that the other fellows will have to get off the earth in the long run, but it will use up plenty of good American soldiers and cost no end of money and anxiety. The only real good that ever comes of such wars is that they develop many clever young officers and make tried-out soldiers for our future use. They are the real schooling grounds for the art of war.

For our part, what we should do is to "declare them banditti." Take off the "closed season" on them, as it were; offer rewards for their heads; put bands of Cuban auxilliary troops after them; stock the old Spanish block-houses with food and grain under our infantry, so that our operations could be fast and continuous, and then go in. The Spanish stayed in their block-houses or only marched a heavy column a day or so outside their own lines. The Cuban guerillas will expect us to do this—whereas they will run midship high on the shoals of error. With our infantry split up into small squads, and put out to form ambuscades all over a province, we could send mounted troops with pack-trains which could be grain-fed from the block-houses on their trail. These grain-fed horses would soon put the riders of the grass-fed ponies afoot. These guerillas would not be able to stop our cavalry by fighting, and if they could be made to fight that would be all we could ask. In running away from our continuous pursuit, they would be at all times liable to run into the constantly shifting infantry ambuscades, which would greatly demoralize them.

This would be a nasty business, but I believe what we have to do could be done better in this way than in any other. It is the old tactics which Miles employed against Geronimo and that old man was a problem in his day. Furthermore let it be remembered that we will see many dark moons before Cuba is rid of bandits.

Santiago Bandits

153

One of Gómez' Men

9. The Sorrows of Don Tomás Pidal, Reconcentrado[1]*

I was driving lately with the great Cuban "war special" Sylvester Scovel along a sun-blazoned road in the Havana province, outside of Marnion; we were away beyond the patrols of the Seventh Corps. The native soldiers pattered along the road on their ratlike ponies. To them Scovel was more than a friend: he was a friend of the great chief Gómez, and that is more than enough for a Cuban.

He pointed to a ditch and to a hill, saying he had been in fights in those places—back in Maceo's time; hot little skirmishes, with no chance to put your hand on your sword. But he had always managed to get away from the Spanish; and so had Maceo—all but the one time.

Beside the road there were fine old mansions—stuccoed brick, with open windows, and with the roofs fallen in. The rank tropic vegetation was fast growing up around them, even now choking the doorways and gravel walks. And the people who lived in them? God knows!

The day grew into noon. We were hungry, and the ardent sun suggested stopping at a village which we were passing through. There was a *fonda*, so we got down from our carriage, and going in, sat down at a table in a little side room.

One is careful about the water in Cuba, and by no chance can a dirty cook get his hands on a boiled egg. We ordered coffee and eggs. A rural Cuban *fonda* is very close to the earth.

Through the open window could be seen the life of the village—men sitting at tables across the way, drinking, smoking, and lazing about. It was Sunday. Little children came to the window and opened their eyes at us, and we pitied their pale anaemic faces and little puffed bellies, for that terrible order of Weyler's had been particularly hard on children. There were men hanging about who looked equally hollow, but very few women.

"Reconcentrados—poor devils," observed my friend.

*Remington's own account.

This harmless peasantry had suffered all that people could suffer. To look at them and to think of them was absolutely saddening. Still, the mass of suffering which they represented also deadened one's sensibilities somewhat, and for an ordinary man to put out his hand in help seemed a thing of no importance.

"I should like to know the personal experiences of one individual of this fallen people, Scovel. I can rise to one man, but two or three hundred thousand people is too big for me."

"All right," replied the alert "special." "We will take that Spanish-looking man over there by the cart. He has been starved, and he is a good type of a Cuban peasant." By the arts of the finished interviewer, Scovel soon had the man sitting at our table, with brandy and water before him. The man's eyes were like live coals, which is the most curious manifestation of starvation. His forehead was wrinkled, the eyebrows drawn up in the middle. He had the greenish pallor which comes when the blood is thin behind a dark coarse skin. He did not seem afraid of us, but behind the listlessness of a low physical condition there was the quick occasional movement of a wild animal.

"Reconcentrado?"

"*Si, señor.* I have suffered beyond counting."

"We are Americans; we sympathize with you; tell us the story of all you have suffered. Your name? Oh! Don Thomás Pidal, will you talk to us?"

"It will be nearly three rains since the King's soldiers burned the thatch over my head and the cavalry shoved us down the road like the beasts.

"I do not know what I shall do. I may yet die—it is a small affair. Everything which I had is now gone. The Americans have come to us; but they should have come long before. At this time we are not worth coming to. Nothing is left but the land, and that the Spaniards could not kill. *Señor,* they of a surety would have burnt it, but that is to them impossible."

"Are you not a Spaniard by birth?"

"No; my father and mother came from over the sea, but I was born in sight of this town. I have always lived here, and I have been happy until the war came. We did not know what the war was like. We used to hear of it years ago, but it was far to the east. The war never came to Punta Brava. We thought it never would; but it did come; and now you cannot see a thatch house or an ox, and you have to gaze hard to see any people in this country about here. That is what war does, *señor,* and we people here did not want war.

156

Fire and Sword in Cuba

"Some of the valiant men who used to dwell around Punta Brava took their guns and the machete of war, and they ran away into the *manigua*. They used to talk in the *fonda* very loud, and they said they would not leave a Spaniard alive on the island. Of a truth, *señor*, many of those *bravos* have gone, they have taken many Spaniards with them to death, and between them both the people who worked in the fields died of the hunger. They ate the oxen, they burned the thatch, and the fields are grown up with bushes. There is not a dog in Punta Brava to-day.

"When the *bravos* ran away, the King's soldiers came into this land in numbers as great as the flies. This village sheltered many of them—many of the battalion San Quintin —and that is why the houses are not flat with the ground."

"Why did you not go out into the *manigua*, Don Pidal?" was asked.

"Oh, *señores*, I am not brave. I never talked loud in the *fonda*. Besides, I had a wife and five children. I lived perfectly. I had a good house of the palm. I had ten cows of fine milk and two yokes of heavy work-oxen. There were ten pigs on my land, and two hundred chickens laid eggs for me. By the sale of these and my fruit I got money. When I killed a pig to sell in Havana, it was thirty dollars. When I did not choose to sell, we had lard in the house for a month, and I had not to buy. Two of my boys, of fourteen and sixteen years, aided me in my work. We bred the beasts, planted tobacco, corn, sweet-potatoes, and plantains, and I had a field of the pineapples, besides many strong mango-trees. Could a man want for what I did not have? We ate twice a day, and even three times. We could have eaten all day if we had so desired.

"Then, *señor*, the tax-gatherers never suspected that I had fourteen hundred dollars in silver buried under the floor of my house. We could work as much as we pleased, or as little; but we worked, *señor*—all the men you see sitting about Punta Brava to-day worked before the war came; not for wages, but for the shame of not doing so. When the yokes were taken from the cattle at night and the fodder was thrown to them, we could divert ourselves. The young men put out on their *guayaberas*, threw their saddles on their *caballitos*, and marched to the girls, where they danced and sang and made love. To get married it was only for the young man to have seventy dollars; the girl had to have only virtue. There was also to go to town to buy, and then the feast-days and the Sunday nights. There was always the work—every day the same, except in the time of tobacco; then we worked into the night. In the house the women washed, they cooked, they looked after the pigs and the chickens, they had the children, and in the time of the tobacco they also went forth into the fields.

158

"It was easy for any man to have money, if he did not put down much on the fighting-cocks. The Church cost much; there was the *cura*, the sacristan—many things to pay away the money for; but even if the goods from Spain did cost a great sum, because the officers of the King made many collections on them, even if the taxes on the land and the annuals were heavy, yet, *señor*, was it not better to pay all than to have the soldiers come? Ah me, *amigo*, of all things the worst are the King's soldiers. It was whispered that the soldiers of your people were bad men. It was said that if they ever came to Punta Brava we would all die; but it is not so. Your soldiers do not live in other people's houses. They are all by themselves in tents up the King's road, and they leave us alone. They do nothing but bring us food in their big wagons. They lied about your soldiers. It was the talk in this country, *señor*, that the great people in the free States of the North wanted to come to us and drive the King's soldiers out of the country, but it was said that your people quarrelled among themselves about coming. The great general who lived in Havana was said to be a friend to all of us, but he did not have the blue soldiers then. He is down the King's road now—I saw him the other day—and a man cannot see over the land far enough to come to the end of his tents.

"If they had been there one day the King's soldiers would not have come through my land and cut my boy to pieces in my own field. They did that, *señor*—cut him with the machetes until he was all over red, and they took many *canastas* of my fruits away. I went to the *comandante* to see what should be done, but he knew nothing about it.

"Then shortly a column of troops came marching by my house, and the officer said by word of mouth that we must all go to town, so that there would be none but rebels in the country. They burned my house and drove all my beasts away—all but one yoke of oxen. I gathered up some of my chickens and what little I could find about the place and put it on a cart, but I could not get my money from the burning house, because they drove us away. This was the first I felt of war.

"I thought that the King would give us food, now that he had taken us from our fields, but we got nothing from the King's officers. I could even then have lived on the outside of the town, with my chickens and what I could have raised, but it was only a short time before the soldiers of the battalion took even my chickens and they made me move inside of a wire fence which ran from one stone fort to another. I tried to get a pass to go outside of the wire fence, and for a few weeks I was used to go and gather what potatoes I could find, but so many men were cut to pieces by the guerillas as they were coming from the fields that I no longer dared go out by day.

"This Was the First I Felt of War."

160

A Spanish Soldier

"We had a little thatch over our heads, but it did not keep out the rain. We became weak with the hunger. We lived in sorrow and with empty bellies. My two young children soon died, and about me many of my friends were dying like dogs. The ox-cart came in the afternoon, and they threw my two children into it like carrion. In that car, *señor*, were twenty-two other dead people. It was terrible. My wife never dried her tears after that. If I had five dollars I could have gotten a box, but I did not have it. The priest would not go for less than double the price of the box, which is the custom. So my two little ones went to Guatoco on an ox-cart loaded with dead like garbage—which the Spanish *comandante* said we were.

"Now came the hard days, *señor*. Not even a dog could pick up enough in Punta Brava to keep life in his ribs. My people lay on the floor of our thatch hut, and they had not the strength to warm water in the kettle. My other child died, and again the ox-cart came. My oldest boy said he was going away and would not return. He got through the wire fence in the dark of the night, and I went with him. We got a small bunch of bananas, and in the black night out there in the *manigua* we embraced each other, and he went away into the country. I have not seen him since; I no longer look for him.

"Only the strongest could live, but I had hopes that by going through the fence every few nights I could keep my wife alive. This I did many times, and came back safely; but I was as careful as a cat, *señor*, as I crawled through the grass, for if a soldier had shot me, my wife would then have but to die. It was hard work to gather the fruit and nuts in the night, and I could not get at all times enough. My wife grew weaker, and I began to despair of saving her. One night I stole some food in a soldier's kettle from near a mess fire, and the men of the battalion fired many shots at me, but without doing me injury. Once a Spanish guerilla, whom I had known before the war came, gave me a piece of fresh beef, which I fed to my wife. I thought to save her with the beef, but she died that night in agony. There was no flesh on her bones.

"Then I ran away through the wire fence. I could not see my wife thrown on the dead wagon, and I never came back until a few days since. I did not care if the guerillas found me. I made my way into Havana, and I got bread from the doorways at times, enough to keep me alive. There was a little work for wages along the docks, but I was not strong to do much. One night I looked between iron bars at some people of your language, *señor*. They were sitting at a table which was covered with food, and when they saw me they gave me much bread, thrusting it out between the bars. A Spaniard would not do that.

162

"And the soldiers fired many shots at me."

For Cuba Libre

"I was not born in a town, and when the King's soldiers sailed away I came back here to my own country. I did not like to live in Havana.

"But now I do not care to live here. I do not see, *señor*, why people who do not want war should have it. I would have paid my taxes. I did not care if the goods from Spain cost much. There was to get along without them if they were beyond price. It was said by the soldiers that we peasants out in the fields told the men of the *manigua* what the battalion San Quintin were doing. *Señor*, the battalion San Quintin did nothing but eat and sleep in Punta Brava. The guerillas roamed about, but I never knew whence they roamed.

"The men of the *manigua* took my potatoes and plantains, but, with their guns and machetes, could I make them not to take them? Was it my fault if fifty armed men did what pleased them?

"*Señor*, why did not the blue soldiers of your language come to us before we died?"

This we were not able to answer.

Appendix

Notes

chapter **1.** Yellow Journalism   1

  1. James Creelman, *On the Great Highway* (New York: Lathrop Publishing Company, 1901).

  2. A. O. Hagen, and E. B. Kaufman, *Cuba at a Glance* (New York: R. H. Russell, 1898), pp. 94–96.

  3. Charles Belmont Davis (ed.), *Adventures and Letters of Richard Harding Davis* (New York: Charles Scribner's Sons, 1917), p. 187.

  4. *Ibid.*, p. 190.

  5. Augustus Thomas, "Recollections of Frederic Remington," *Century Magazine*, July, 1913, p. 357.

  6. *Ibid.*

  7. Frederic Remington, "Under Which King?" *Collier's Weekly*, April 8, 1899.

  8. Original letter in the collection of Remington's correspondence with Poultney Bigelow. Courtesy St. Lawrence University, Canton, New York.

  9. Augustus Thomas, "Recollections of Frederic Remington," *Century Magazine*, July, 1913, p. 356.

chapter **2.** The Training of Cavalry   29

  1. *Harper's Weekly*, April 2, 1898.

chapter **3.** Seagoing Plainsman   37

    1. A. O. Hagen, and E. B. Kaufman, *Cuba at a Glance* (New York: R. H. Russell, 1898), pp. 95–100.

chapter **4.** Tampa—the Wait for Action   56

    1. Richard Harding Davis, *The Cuban and Porto Rican Campaigns* (New York: Charles Scribner's Sons, 1898), p. 56.

    2. *Ibid.*

    3. *Ibid.*

    4. Charles Belmont Davis, *Adventures and Letters of Richard Harding Davis* (New York: Charles Scribner's Sons, 1917), p. 192.

chapter **5.** With the Fifth Corps   74

    1. Frederic Remington, "With the Fifth Corps," *Harper's Monthly Magazine*, November, 1898.

    2. Frederic Remington, "How the Horses Died," *Harper's Weekly*, July 15, 1899.

chapter **6.** Heroic Americans   118

    1. *Collier's Weekly*, April 7, 1900.

chapter **7.** The Bronco Buster   132

    1. Augustus Thomas, "Recollections of Frederic Remington," *Century Magazine*, July, 1913, p. 361.

    2. Theodore Roosevelt, *The Rough Riders* (New York: Charles Scribner's Sons, 1899).

Glossary

Bunco—swindle

Caballitos—small horses

Cabanas (*Cabañas*)—small houses, cabins

Canastas—baskets

Doughboy—infantryman

Dragonnade—a rapid, devastating incursion

Fice (Feist)—mongrel

Fonda—plaza

Guayaberas—elegant shirts

Guerillas—irregular troops employed by the Spaniards

Guidon—small flag or pennant

Guyed—mocked

Hardtack—hard biscuit or bread made only with flour and water

Jackies—landsman's nickname for a seaman, resented by the latter

Manigua—thicket, jungle

Reconcentrado—displaced person of war

Remounts—horses not previously ridden or handled

Shotted—loaded with ammunition

Span—trim; currently used in conjunction with "spick"

Yellowleg—cavalryman; reference to yellow stripe worn down trouser
leg on uniform

Index

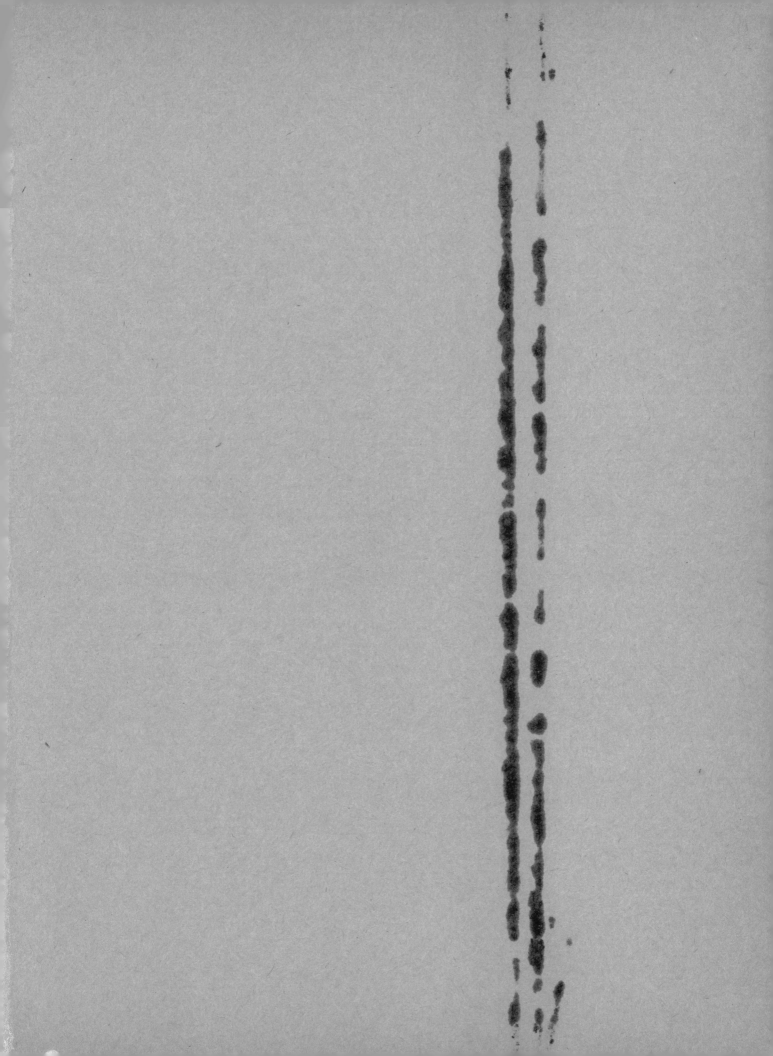